PROBLEMS OF MODERN GOVERNMENT

Private Life and Public Order

PROBLEMS OF MODERN GOVERNMENT

General Editor: THEODORE J. LOWI, *University of Chicago*

Each volume in this series examines
questions of public policy within their
political context

PRIVATE LIFE AND PUBLIC ORDER

PUBLIC POLICIES AND THEIR POLITICS

THE POLITICS OF EDUCATION

Private Life and

Public Order

THE CONTEXT OF MODERN PUBLIC POLICY

Edited with an introduction by   3 ⊱

THEODORE J. LOWI

UNIVERSITY OF CHICAGO

NEW YORK

W · W · NORTON & COMPANY · INC ·

"Aristocracy in a Democracy" from: Alexis de Tocqueville, *Democracy in America,*
translated by Phillips Bradley. Copyright 1945 by Alfred A. Knopf, Inc. Reprinted by
permission.

"The Democratic Mold" from: David Truman, *The Governmental Process.* Copyright
1951 by Alfred A. Knopf, Inc. Reprinted by permission.

"Letter from Birmingham Jail" from: Martin Luther King, Jr., *Why We Can't Wait.*
Copyright © 1963 by Martin Luther King, Jr. Reprinted by permission of Harper & Row,
Publishers.

"Natural Harmony in a Freely Competitive Society" from: Ludwig von Mises, *Human
Action, Revised Edition.* Reprinted by permission of Henry Regnery Co.

"The Great Society and the Loss of Self-regulation" from: Karl Mannheim, *Freedom,
Power, and Democratic Planning.* Copyright 1950 by Oxford University Press, Inc. Reprinted by permission.

"The Internal Difficulties of Democracy" from: Ernest Barker, *Reflections on Government.* Copyright 1942 by Oxford University Press, Inc. Reprinted by permission.

"Came the Revolution" from: John Kenneth Galbraith, "Came the Revolution: Rise of
an Orthodoxy" in *The New York Times Book Review,* May 16, 1965. © 1965 by The
New York Times Company. Reprinted by permission.

"The Rule of Law" from: F. A. Hayek, *Road to Serfdom.* Reprinted by permission of
The University of Chicago Press.

"The Roosevelt Revolution" from: Mario Einaudi, *The Roosevelt Revolution,* © 1959 by
Mario Einaudi. Reprinted by permission of Harcourt, Brace & World, Inc.

"The Making of the Issues—1964" from: Theodore H. White, *The Making of the President—1964.* Copyright © 1965 by Theodore H. White. Reprinted by permission of the
author and Atheneum Publishers.

Library of Congress Catalog Card No. 67-11085
Printed in the United States of America
1 2 3 4 5 6 7 8 9 0

Contents

Introduction

THE PHRASE "private life and public order" expresses two different ways of looking at the same thing: society in its effort to provide and to survive. In the real world it is impossible to separate private from public spheres. Analytically a distinction must be made between them, but only the better to assess their interconnections in the real world. "Private life and public order" is a statement of intimate relationship.

The phrase also implies a problem. Private life and public order will always be at odds. Every effort to establish and maintain some ideal relation between them is matched by other efforts making certain that success will never be more than temporary. Adjustments in philosophy and religion have allowed modern man to accept happiness without guilt. Out of this the individual in modern democratic societies has developed urges to reject his discomforts. Ultimately he perceives some relation between his discomfort and the environment that is beyond his immediate control, and he tends to group together with others as they discover they share the same irritants. Sooner or later they also begin to agree on the specific causes of their distress. It matters all too little whether they are correct or justified in their diagnosis.

Through their common irritants people become "factions." With factions—or interest groups and parties as we call them today—the political process has begun. So has public disorder. Factions are mischievous to public order. But we cannot rid ourselves of them. We would not want to if we could. "Liberty," goes Madison's famous axiom, "is to faction what air is to fire." The cure for faction is worse than the disease.

The organization of free individuals into factions, groups and parties produces friction between the basic components of private life and public order—*that is, friction between the economy and the state*. We can define the economy narrowly to mean production and exchange of goods and services; or we can define it to mean virtually all private activity outside the living room. Either way, economic forces work themselves out in the long run. But politics works in the short run. Private systems of activity may indeed yield an acceptable public order, in the long run. But factions form precisely against the long run. The unemployed get hungry waiting for unencumbered industrial conditions to right themselves. Automation is perceived by today's unionist as a threat to himself; whether justified or not, he may also feel that without action now his children may never be born to realize the future benefits of automation. Small businessmen and farmers were never ones to wait for monopolies to break up from their own weaknesses.

This is not to suggest that the difference between private life and public order is the difference between bad and good or good and bad. Long run versus short run is a distinction more truly between the objective and the subjective. In the Western democracies this comes down to a hard, practical distinction between *rights* and *legitimacy*. Both are essential to our society, yet neither is maintained and fostered the same way: The *rights* underlying private action depend very heavily upon property values. These are not always tangible, but they tend to be measurable and known quantities. That has been the secret of their attractiveness to the rational Western man. *Legitimacy* is a sum of feelings. It is that sense of the rightness of the overall public condition; it is a sum of the propensities of people to accept that extremely ambiguous condition as a good thing. Without timely response to organized expressions against certain aspects of that condition, government could lose its claim as the source of legitimacy. As long as political leaders see their own power, as well as the very legitimacy of the government itself, as resting upon ability to respond quickly to all hard-pressed demands, there will be pressure toward expansion of government every time society requires adjustment.

There are fundamental issues here, and they will be with us forever. In a democracy there is a tendency toward expansion of the public sphere, but no expansion can be shown *a priori* to be desirable *or* undesirable. Do democratic regimes legitimize themselves only through positive responses in new programs, or is that just a fashionable contemporary myth? Does each and every public policy produce an increment of public order, or have some forms of government action proven to be patently bad for public order? Are there any social problems that would be better solved if left alone, or would none go away without conscious, administrative attention? Even when public order is produced by a public policy, is the price paid too great in loss of individual character and self-reliance? Finally, are all these questions beside the point in a democracy? When we make our choice for democracy do we also choose never to consider limiting what that democracy chooses to do? Are there, in other words, any limits that can rightfully be put upon the reach of democratic governments; or must democracy by its very nature be left entirely to its own wisdom? And, if the reach of democratic government is unlimited, are there even any procedures and means of control that are off limits?

Clear-cut answers can be found only at the extremes. On the one side the answer implies that there are values one must put above democracy and, therefore, that some antidemocratic elites must be set up to guide and husband democracy in order to save it from itself. On the other side the answer may seem more consistent to the ardent believer in democracy, but that answer can be the beginning of a commitment to a most frightening prospect, the twentieth-century absolutism of people's tyranny.

These issues are not outmoded or old-fashioned. Momentary consensus in America has overshadowed debate that had enlivened public opinion in times past. But that consensus is superficial and temporary. The issues and the debates will emerge again as times and leaders change. They will emerge again because each generation upsets the apple cart one way or another and must then face all the alternatives in setting it up again. Furthermore, the issues will reemerge because it is an American culture trait to be preoccupied with the proper role government is to play in maintaining public order. In the past we have been preoccupied to an extent most foreign observers find ludicrous.

Preoccupation with the role of government in adjusting private life to public order was only natural in a country so rich in the

means for individual and nongovernmental solutions. That attitude was to a great extent a reflection of the enormous success
of the industrializing economy in finding its own ways out of its
own problems. Moreover, the strength of that preoccupation—
the strength of belief in the principle of *laissez-faire*—actually
contributed to the maintenance of an astonishingly small governmental sphere for the first hundred years of our history. Supreme
Court Justice Oliver Wendell Holmes vowed in his dissent in
Lochner v. New York (*see below*) that the American Constitution
did not enact Herbert Spencer's *Social Statics*. Mr. Holmes'
aphorism was good prophecy, but it was terrible history. Herbert
Spencer, a Darwinian extremist among *laissez-faire* popularizers,
believed that government intervention was contrary to the laws
of nature in that it protected the weak from their fate against the
fittest; thereby, and despite its best intentions, government intervention slowed the evolution of the superior man and the health-
ier society. Extreme, yes; unrepresentative, no. The prevailing
ideology in the nineteenth century and beyond, and also the
prevailing constitutional doctrine (as expressed by the *majority*
of the Court in the Lochner case) was that government is a necessary evil and that any expansion beyond the minimum comes
ultimately at the expense of individual rights as well as future
public order.

At the federal level this attitude applied with particular
strength. Government influence was confined (throughout the
nineteenth century) very largely to two types of activities. There
was, first, the judicial determination of "cases and controversies"
arising out of private initiative involving private rights and
damages. Second, there was the relatively passive public economic
activity of patronage, literally of government as patron, expressed in internal improvements, subsidies, land grants and
tariffs. Government influence was more than negligible, but it
tended to be geared toward fostering the economic dynamism of
the country without directing it or interfering with it.

Ideology and social problems both began to change after the
turn of the century with the end of the frontier, the establishment
of a single, continental market, the commercialization of agriculture, the emergence of large-scale industry and large proletariat,

and the mechanization and urbanization of almost everything and everybody. The problems of public order were bound to change—with or without the assistance of a change in ideology. Still, the response in new governmental activity was not immediate. As late as 1914, fitful responses to economic distress and large-scale social upheaval and protest included: a clumsy arrangement for attacking monopoly and monopolistic practices (the Sherman Antitrust Act), a more specialized mechanism for attacking the railroads as a special sort of monopoly (the Interstate Commerce Commission), some laws and arrangements for combating interstate crime (against transporting stolen children, automobiles, and sawed-off shotguns but not against the products of child labor or substandard factories), and a semi-public cooperative venture in making currency and credit more elastic (the Federal Reserve System). Domestic requirements for prosecuting World War I accelerated the pace of change, but a truly new type of government did not come into obvious and undeniable existence until the 1930s, with the efforts of the Roosevelt Administration to combat the Great Depression.

All of the new socio-economic forces, all of the changes in ideology, and all of the pressure on the established doctrine controlling the size and scope of government came to a critical juncture in 1937. The official judicial doctrines, still not unconnected with Herbert Spencer's *Social Statics,* had led the Supreme Court to a series of spectacular decisions voiding fundamental enactments of the New Deal. Popular pressure, presidential pressure, a timely change of membership, and a change of heart of one Justice ("the switch in time that saved nine"), combined to bring about a constitutional revolution. The Constitutional Revolution of 1937 played a part in the creation of, but was also in part a reflection of, a modern state. The "new constitution" comprehends extension of federal authority to almost anything that the democratic political process sees fit to reach. The modern state, for a generation after 1937, was based upon the principle and practices of positive government—of government seen as a good force with occasional bad effects rather than a bad force that occasionally could not be avoided. At the national level, positive government meant, above all, establishment of an insurance state—dedication of new and coordination of old policies toward the erection of a floor against societal disaster.

The insurance state was, however, only the first major result of the new "constitution." There has been still another revolution in government since 1937, although its importance may be overlooked because no formal event or decision marks it. An accumulation of responses to the problems of our time transformed national government by translating the notion of positive government into government with a definite obligation to act—an obligation to prevent and to create rather than merely to shield and to react. The second revolution is creating a welfare state on top of the insurance state. National government became charged, for better or worse, with responsibility for maximization of opportunity rather than erection of minimal protections. Less stress came to be put upon societal disaster, more upon individual well-being within a healthy society. The attitude of the average citizen and group has changed to such an extent that each is more likely than not to turn to government at first rather than at last. The attitude of the average leader is that all human needs define rights, that rights are, therefore, numerous, and that for every right there must be a remedy.

The year 1957 can be seen as a turning point toward the second revolution. It was the year of Sputnik, and it was the year of Little Rock. These two events, more than any others, precipitated the crisis of public authority and helped define the purposes of public action for the years to come. The second revolution had been emerging slowly since 1946, with the passage of the Employment Act, which made the federal government responsible for maintaining a steady economy at all times. It was set loose officially but with little immediate effect by the historic civil rights decision of 1954 *(Brown v. Board of Education)*. After 1957 the new and compelling agenda of public order had been established. With increasing clarity since that time the relatively static notions of insurance, security, and freedom from restraint gave way to the dynamic and positive compulsions of expanding individual opportunity, initiatives in securing rights, liberties and equality, and investments in human and community resources. New standards sprang from these new characterizations of public problems, and those standards suddenly spotlighted an overwhelming backlog of pressing need and insufficient action.

The first revolution was very largely successful. That is, the constitutional and governmental responses proved to be acceptable approaches to the problems, and the insurance state became established fact. It is hard to imagine the country without deposit insurance, social security in its many forms, and the several basic counter-cyclical mechanisms for security against extreme economic fluctuations. It is, however, too early to tell about the second revolution. Grappling with the outward symptoms of maladjustment in modern society has revealed the complexity of the underlying intangible and human causes.

The political responses that constitute the second revolution to date have been numerous, well-financed, and often well conceived from the economic and administrative standpoint. Thus, for example, the Office of Education in 1957 was a minor service agency with $174 million to spend on elementary and secondary education throughout the country. In 1967, the Office of Education is responsible for awesome enforcement functions under civil rights and cold war legislation, plus a budget for elementary and secondary education alone of over $1.5 billion. Health services and research expenditures by the federal government trebled between fiscal 1957 and 1962, and then trebled still again between fiscal 1962 and 1967. A large-scale and continuing War on Poverty was inconceivable before 1957, except as an emergency device during a depression. These combine with an enormous expansion of the personnel and expenditures of programs established after 1937. But neither money nor personnel fully measure the extent of the change. It is necessary to appreciate those smaller agencies, such as the Federal Reserve Board, the Atomic Energy Commission, the Internal Revenue Service, the Federal Bureau of Investigation, and the Civil Rights Division of the Justice Department, which exercise vast powers over persons and property. The growth of the number and the activities of these agencies, along with the new and incredible technology of detection, of investigation, of control, and of legal violence, put mid-twentieth-century government into stark contrast even to government in 1937, not to mention 1907 or 1877.

The decade since the beginning of the civil rights revolution, the education revolution, and the technological and scientific revolution has thus been an exhilarating political decade, culminating in the most active, legislating Congress since the first 100 days of Franklin Roosevelt's Administration. Government action in the 1960s proves that the political apparatus of our democracy responds quickly to disorder once the legal and constitutional barriers to its response have been lowered.

So, as modern liberals and humanitarians would have it, the polity has finally been allowed to intervene without being required to wait for the long-run to arrive. Yet we witness continuing and increasing evidence of declining legitimacy of public authority along with the further weakening of informal controls of family, neighborhood and groups.

We witness governmental effort of gigantic proportion to solve problems forthwith and directly. Yet we witness expressions of personal alienation increasing in frequency and intensity.

We witness a vast expansion of effort to bring the ordinary citizen into closer rapport with the democratic process, including unprecedented efforts to confer upon the poor and uneducated the power to make official decisions involving their own fate. Yet at the very same time we witness crisis after crisis in the very institutions in which the new methods of decision-making seemed most appropriate.

It is as though each new program or program expansion were admission of prior governmental inadequacy or failure without necessarily being a contribution to order and well-being. The War on Poverty programs have become as often as not instruments of social protest. Riots of a type witnessed in the Watts district of Los Angeles, the movements for civilian police review boards and ombudsmen in many cities, the sit-ins and marches even where no specifically evil laws are being enforced against a special race or group, the strikes and protests by civil servants, nurses, doctors, transport and defense workers, and others in vital occupations, new political parties on extremes of Right and Left—all these and many others are evidence of increasing impatience with established ways of resolving social conflict and dividing up society's prized values. Verbal and organizational attacks on that vague being, the "power structure," even in cities with histories of strong reform movements and imaginative social programs, reflect increasing rejection of pluralistic patterns in favor of more direct prosecution of claims against society. Many of these new patterns and problems may have been generated by racial issues, but it is clear that the crisis in race relations was only a precipitant. The ironic fact is that the post-1937 political economy had produced unprecedented prosperity, but that as the national output increased arithmetically, the rate of rising expectations seems to have shot up geometrically—in a modern expression of the Malthusian Law. Public authority, partly due to political promises, partly due to the new Keynesian economics, partly due to some natural turning to government by those who were left out of the prosperity, was left to grapple with this alienating gap between expectations and reality.

The woeful imperfection of contemporary efforts to use government as a force for public order is equaled only by the astonishment of enlightened observers at the spectacle that alienation seems to be growing with prosperity and public services. That spectacle proves conclusively that nothing is cut and dried about the relation between private life and public order. The many unanticipated consequences of our most heralded new programs will always stand as a reminder of how little we really know about the role government can best play in producing the conditions for public order. There has been enormous progress in the past generation in our understanding of the modern economy, and there is at least some progress in theory and research on politics and government. But this kind of progress never seems to catch up with social change. If the assumptions about man and society upon which eighteenth century philosophers and statesmen operated seem quaint, optimistic and uninformed to us today, so also must our own to our children if not already to ourselves. We must inevitably hear the echoes of our angry derision of Herbert Hoover.

This very ignorance of the true determinants of individual behavior and the uncertainty about the constants underlying public order have given rise in every preceding generation to ideologies of one sort or another. Ideologies are general statements of "is and ought" which can be called upon to justify one or another course of action. Once adopted, a course of action sets in motion counter-ideologies and alternative approaches to public order and public policy. This is why the "consensus of the 1960s" is neither a permanent nor a particularly healthy condition. No viable society and no intelligent leadership can long exist without returning regularly to debate upon the premises of public policy.

The inevitable shortcomings of any course of action have led to innovations and spurts of debate over issues of public policy. However, all of these occur within a very stable context of general values that underlie and surround timely ideologies and fashionable proposals. In essence this context extends back throughout the history of political philosophy and enlightened statecraft; in present form this context has been with us throughout most of the modern industrial period. But since surface manifestations do change with the influence of new regimes and dynamic leaders, they may also mislead and confuse. In the heat of debate, underlying premises are frequently neglected, often deliberately hidden. Thus through superficial treatment by politicians and the modern news media a man can, according to Shaw, become opinionated without becoming educated. In America, pragmatism has all too often been used as an excuse for superficiality.

This volume is an effort to provide that essential context for modern public policy. It is an effort to identify the perennial problems underlying contemporary ideologies, alternatives, and issues. The readings were selected and organized around a very limited number of broad but highly selective questions, and these in turn arise out of experience with the political process.

The volume is organized in three parts. Each part corresponds to a fairly distinct phase of the political process and to an identifiable category of values in political and sociological theory. Part One begins with the individual as the unit and attempts to identify, through classic expressions in the literature, the issues regarding the individual's freedoms and their consequences. In Part Two, the readings proceed to the institutions and practices that are the sources of nongovernmental control. Successful institutions shape the individual, to make his wishes as congruent as possible with social needs, to control the individual when his wishes are not congruent. These institutions also may, or may not, maintain the individual in his freedom. But they must provide some degree of elemental public order or no form of government could succeed. In other words, Part Two is a debate on the conditions of "private self-government." Part Three is devoted to evaluation of the various forms of governmental control that Americans have resorted to, sometimes because of and sometimes in spite of doctrines pertaining to the proper role of government.

The best way to bring all of these broad and abstract questions into direct focus upon the readings is to provide the rationale which guided their selection and their organization.

PRIVATE LIFE: FREEDOMS, RESTRAINTS, AND CONSEQUENCES

What forms of action are available to the individual and of what consequences to himself and to society are his choices? In the classic Western view, the freely acting individual is not a problem of disorder as long as he pursues his enlightened self-interest. To Adam Smith, and to the many thinkers influenced by him, private life *is* public order. Institutions *may* interfere with, rather than contribute to, the "wealth of nations," or any other measure of public good. At a different level the same thinking holds true for Madison, whose system of self-interested factions was deemed to be largely as automatic a regulator as Smith's self-interested entrepreneur. This "Madisonian Model" (now generally called pluralism) is still very much a part of modern thought, especially among political scientists. Lincoln's approach is not antithetical. He simply attempts to state a particular condition upon which ultimately rests both the Smithian and the Madisonian view of the concordance of freedom and order: Obedience to all laws must be part of the very meaning of *enlightened* self-interest.

For each of these fundamental theses there is an equally serious dissent. All three dissents—those of Tocqueville, Michels-Truman, and King—have one common thread of argument. Each agrees that economic and political freedoms can produce public order as well as personal satisfaction, *but not necessarily at an accepta-*

ble level of equilibrium. Tocqueville by brilliant extrapolation, and Michels and Truman by astute observation, find inequality and suppression as the possible consequences of free activity, largely because of the severely oligarchic character of so many of the organizations that arise out of the very free and rational pursuit of wealth or power. The Negro community also stands as an example of the fact that neither economic nor political equality may be generated naturally out of free economic or political competition. The experience of the American Negro is also grounds for Martin Luther King's dissent from Lincoln: If law is at all an expression of the needs of earlier "power structures," then Lincoln's call for obedience may not liberate but could perpetuate an unequal system.

Three classic expressions of the need and desirability of enlightened economic and political freedom are juxtaposed with three serious dissents. These dissents are not to economic or political freedom as such, for such dissents are altogether outside the American political tradition. Rather they are dissents to the claim that the solution to any freedom is simply more freedom. Together these six views are not meant to identify "problems" for which we are to search for appropriate "solutions." They identify perennial and fundamental values—the poles of practicable choice. They are a substantial part of the framework within which each generation must make choices for the amount and type of public order it is going to produce for itself.

PUBLIC ORDER: INSTITUTIONS IN CAPITALIST SOCIETY

To what extent is modern society self-governing and without need of the coercive assistance of government? No society can operate without being self-regulative to a great extent. No conceivable government, particularly in open societies, could succeed in maintaining public order if it were burdened with handling on a regular basis more than a miniscule proportion of all possible human and group problems. The first question then is how much is left and can be left to the normal workings of non-governmental institutions? Only then can we ask how much can and should be assumed by the authoritative and non-voluntary operation of government.

The answers, though many, all rest upon diagnosis of economic and other social processes and their effectiveness in producing public order. The major issue in modern society in this respect is capitalism, its related institutions, and their impact on other institutions and human beings. Due to the problem of space in the volume, institutions that are not strictly speaking capitalistic or in any way economic are covered, but largely in the context of the impact of capitalism. Weber and Mannheim offer an important introduction to basic hypotheses on the social origins and consequences of an industrializing society. Von Mises dissents in a way to make it difficult for anyone to be led too easily by Weber and Mannheim to facile conclusions about the need for government to provide for capitalistic weaknesses. Barker and Swift, on the other hand, suggest that there may be little choice about intervention. Barker sees government being pulled in by the confrontation of ideologies and social forces, regardless of beliefs to the contrary. Swift's ironies suggest that every government decision is interventionistic and discriminatory anyway, and that our only choice has to do with what kind of intervention we prefer.

PUBLIC ORDER: THE ROLE OF GOVERNMENT IN AMERICA

Diagnosis and debate turn from institutions in the private sector to those of government—but with the same ends in view: How vital is government to public order? How much need is there for invoking the legitimate, coercive powers of the state? How much need is there now in relation to earlier times? Are there any basic problems in the use of these powers that we should face but have not?

Even the most orthodox *laissez-faire* position would concede to government a few essential functions, such as adjudication and sanitation. Others go a step or two further and concede to government a role wherever a problem involves questions of benefits or liabilities to the whole community; examples include the size of the defense establishment, the value of currency, certain basic public works, whose impact cannot be apportioned according to specific individual preferences. On the other hand, those who doubt that freedom is ever self-governing or self-generating, or who doubt that the private institutions of capitalism or community or competing groups are ever sufficient, opt for varying degrees of governmental "supplement" for maintaining order and expanding well-being. For better or worse, the range of disagreement has never been as great in the United States as elsewhere. Socialism—public ownership of all capitalistic property—has never been and still is not an acceptable alternative (and is not debated in this volume). The range of effective disagreement in the United States is narrower still since the Constitutional Revolution of 1937, when Holmes' *Lochner* dissent became the opinion of the majority (of the Supreme Court and the country). However, serious issues still exist and will continue to: How large is the governmental sector supposed to be? This rests almost entirely upon one's diagnosis of the problems set forth and debated in Parts One and Two. How positive should government policy be? Government scope can be quite large but passive, as in the nineteenth century, and as anticipated in Hamilton's Report. Or it can be active but negative, as in the early regulation at issue in the Lochner case—a series of thou-shalt-nots. Or it can be as the regulation developed in the twentieth century, actively and positively directing conduct in civil rights, in mass communications, and so on. This is exemplified in the selection on Civil Rights. Or it can be active and positive through manipulation of the entire system rather than the people in it, as in fiscal and monetary control, where the very environment of conduct is influenced. Galbraith and Kennedy express such views.

Finally, does majoritarian government, committed as it is to equality, tend, like the Frankenstein monster, to impair the very freedoms that created it? Do policies that are justified as treatments of social ills reduce the capacity of society and individuals to treat themselves? Smith and Mises represent fundamental concerns on this point. Are there any built-in controls in a democracy that prevent its government from extending itself without warrant to all realms of private life and public order? The Supreme Court feels, as in the Barnette case, that some elitist guidance is unavoidable in a democracy. Are democratic governments likely to kick over the traces when faced with an emergency? Barker offers some worthy observations. Einaudi's is a classic and hopeful essay. Would it be all that bad if our government were guided entirely by popular rule? Hayek offers a warning that was heeded by old-fashioned nineteenth century liberals but must also be heeded by twentieth century liberals who now are making the choices for the kind of public order the next generation is going to enjoy. Has our big society with its great needs and complex government lost its capacity to deal with Hayek's issue or any of the great issues? White's brilliant account of the 1964 Presidential campaign provides a partially hopeful answer and suggests that the revival of the great issues for the next round of debate has already begun.

PROBLEMS OF MODERN GOVERNMENT

Private Life and Public Order

once under the view of the spectator. In those great manufactures, on the contrary, which are destined to supply the great wants of the great body of the people, every different branch of the work employs so great a number of workmen, that it is impossible to collect them all into the same workhouse. We can seldom see more, at one time, than those employed in one single branch. Though in such manufactures, therefore, the work may really be divided into a much greater number of parts than in those of a more trifling nature, the division is not near so obvious, and has accordingly been much less observed.

To take an example, therefore, from a very trifling manufacture, but one in which the division of labour has been very often taken notice of, the trade of the pin-maker, a workman not educated to this business (which the division of labour has rendered a distinct trade), nor acquainted with the use of the machinery employed in it (to the invention of which the same division of labour has probably given occasion), could scarce, perhaps, with his utmost industry, make one pin in a day, and certainly could not make twenty. But, in the way in which this business is now carried on, not only the whole work is a peculiar trade, but it is divided into a number of branches, of which the greater part are likewise peculiar trades. One man draws out the wire, another straights it, a third cuts it, a fourth points it, a fifth grinds in at the top for receiving the head; to make the head requires two or three distinct operations; to put it on is a peculiar business, to whiten the pins is another; it is even a trade by itself to put them into the paper; and the important business of making a pin is, in this manner, divided into about eighteen distinct operations, which, in some manufactories, are all performed by distinct hands, though in others the same man will sometimes perform two or three of them. I have seen a small manufactory of this kind where ten men only were employed, and where some of them, consequently, performed two or three distinct operations. But though they were very poor, and, therefore, but indifferently accommodated with the necessary machinery, they could, when they exerted themselves, make among them about twelve pounds of pins in a day. There are in a pound upwards of four thousand pins of a middling size. Those ten persons, therefore, could make among them upwards of forty-eight thousand pins in a day. Each person, therefore, making a tenth part of forty-eight thousand pins, might be considered as making four thousand eight hundred pins in a day. But if they had all wrought separately and independently, and without any of them having been educated to this peculiar business, they certainly could not each of them have made twenty, perhaps not one, pin in a day; that is, certainly, not the two hundred and fortieth, perhaps not the four thousand eight hundredth, part of what they are at present capable of performing, in consequence of a proper division and combination of their different operations.

In every other art and manufacture the effects of the division of labour are similar to what they are in this very trifling one; though, in many of them, the labour can neither be so much subdivided, nor reduced to so great a simplicity of operation. The division of labour, however, so far as it can be introduced, occasions, in every art, a proportionable increase of the productive powers of labour. The separation of different trades and employments from one another, seems to have taken place in consequence of this advantage. This separation, too, is generally carried furthest in those countries which employ the highest degree of industry and improvement; what is the work of one man in a rude state of society being generally that of several in an improved one. In every improved society, the farmer is generally nothing but a farmer, the manufacturer nothing but a manufacturer. The labour, too, which is necessary to produce any one complete manufacture is almost always divided among a great number of hands. . . .

This great increase of the quantity of work, which, in consequence of the division of labour, the same number of people are capable of performing, is owing to three different circumstances; first, to the increase of dexterity in every particular workman; secondly, to the saving of the time which is commonly lost in passing from one species of work to another; and, lastly, to the invention of a great number of machines which facilitate and abridge labour, and enable one man to do the work of many. . . .

It is the great multiplication of the productions of all the different arts, in consequence of the division of labour, which occasions, in a well-governed society, that universal opulence which extends itself to the lowest ranks of the people. Every workman has a great quantity of his own work to dispose of, beyond what he himself has occasion for; and, every other workman being exactly in the same situation, he is enabled to exchange a great quantity of his own goods for a great quantity, or, what comes to the same thing, for the price of a great quantity of theirs. He supplies them abundantly with what they have occasion for, and they accommodate him as amply with what he has occasion for, and a general plenty diffuses itself through all the different ranks of the society.

Observe the accommodation of the most common artificer or day-labourer in a civilised and thriving country, and you will perceive, that the number of people of whose industry a part, though but a small part, has been employed in procuring him this accommodation, exceeds all computation . . . What a variety of labour, too, is necessary in order to produce the tools of the meanest of those workmen! To say nothing of such complicated machines as the ship of the sailor, the mill of the fuller, or even the loom of the weaver, let us consider, only, what a variety of labour is requisite, in order to form that very simple machine the shears, with which the shepherd clips the wool. The miner, the builder of the furnace for smelting the ore, the feller of the timber, the burner of the charcoal, to be made use of in the smelting-house, the brickmaker, the bricklayer, the workmen who attend the furnace, the millwright, the forger, the smith, must all of them join their different arts in order to produce them. Were we to examine, in the same manner, all the different parts of his dress and household furniture, the coarse linen shirt which he wears next his skin, the shoes which cover his feet, the bed which he lies on, and all the different parts which compose it, the kitchen-grate at which he prepares his victuals, the coals which he makes use of for that purpose, dug from the bowels of the earth, and brought to him perhaps by a long sea and a long land carriage, all the other utensils of his kitchen, all the furniture of his table, the knives and forks, the earthen or pewter plates upon which he serves up and divides his victuals, the different hands employed in preparing his bread and his beer, the glass window which lets in the heat and the light, and keeps out the wind and the rain, with all the knowledge and art requisite for preparing that beautiful and happy invention, without which these northern parts of the world could scarce have afforded a very comfortable habitation, together with the tools of all the different workmen employed in producing those different conveniences; if we examine, I say, all these things, and consider what a variety of labour is employed about each of them, we shall be sensible that, without the assistance and cooperation of many thousands, the very meanest person in a civilised country could not be provided, even according to, what we very falsely imagine, the easy and simple manner in which he is commonly accommodated. Compared, indeed, with the more extravagant luxury of the great, his accommodation must no doubt appear extremely simple and easy; and yet it may be true, perhaps, that the accommodation of an European prince does not always so much exceed that of an industrious and frugal peasant, as the accommodation of the latter exceeds that of many an African king, the absolute master of the lives and liberties of ten thousand naked savages.

Of the Principle Which Gives Occasion to the Division of Labour • This division of labour, from which so many advantages are derived, is not originally the effect of any human wisdom, which foresees and intends that general opulence to which it gives occasion. It is the necessary, though very slow and gradual, consequence of a certain propensity in human nature which has in view no such extensive utility, the propensity to truck, barter, and exchange one thing for another.

Whether this propensity be one of those original principles in human nature, of which no further account can be given, or whether, as seems more probable, it be the necessary consequence of the faculties of reason and speech, it belongs not to our present subject to inquire. It is common to all men, and to be found in no other race of animals, which seem to know neither this nor any other species of contracts. . . . In most every other race of animals, each individual, when it is grown up to maturity, is entirely independent, and in its natural state has occasion for the assistance of no other living creature; but man has almost con-

stant occasion for the help of his brethren, and it is in vain for him
to expect it from their benevolence only. He will be more likely
to prevail, if he can interest their self-love in his favour, and show
them that it is for their own advantage to do for him what he requires of them. Whoever offers to another a bargain of any kind
proposes to do this. Give me that which I want, and you shall
have this which you want, is the meaning of every such offer;
and it is in this manner that we obtain from one another the far
greater part of those good offices which we stand in need of. It
is not from the benevolence of the butcher, the brewer, or the
baker, that we expect our dinner, but from their regard to their
own interest. We address ourselves, not to their humanity but to
their self-love, and never talk to them of our own necessities but
of their advantages. Nobody but a beggar chooses to depend
chiefly upon the benevolence of his fellow citizens. Even a beggar does not depend upon it entirely. The charity of well-dis-
posed people, indeed supplies him with the whole fund of his
subsistence. But though this principle ultimately provides him
with all the necessaries of life which he has occasion for, it neither
does nor can provide him with them as he has occasion for them.
The greater part of his occasional wants are supplied in the same
manner as those of other people, by treaty, by barter, and by
purchase. With the money which one man gives him he pur-
chases food. The old clothes which another bestows upon him,
he exchanges for other old clothes which suit him better, or for
lodging, or for food, or for money, with which he can buy either
food, clothes, or lodging, as he has occasion.

As it is by treaty, by barter, and by purchase that we obtain
from one another the greater part of those mutual good offices
which we stand in need of, so it is this same trucking disposition
which originally gives occasion to the division of labour. In a
tribe of hunters or shepherds, a particular person makes bows
and arrows, for example, with more readiness and dexterity than
any other. He frequently exchanges them for cattle or for venison
with his companions; and he finds, at last, that he can in this
manner get more cattle and venison than if he himself went to the
field to catch them. From a regard to his own interest, therefore,
the making of bows and arrows grows to be his chief business,

and he becomes a sort of armourer.... The certainty of being able to exchange all that surplus part of the produce of his own labour, which is over and above his own consumption, for such parts of the produce of other men's labour as he may have occasion for, encourages every man to apply himself to a particular occupation, and to cultivate and bring to perfection whatever talent or genius he may possess for that particular species of business.

The difference of natural talents in different men is, in reality, much less than we are aware of; and the very different genius which appears to distinguish men of different professions, when grown up to maturity, is not, upon many occasions, so much the cause as the effect of the division of labour.... By nature, a philosopher is not in genius and disposition half so different from a street porter, as a mastiff is from a greyhound, or a greyhound from a spaniel, or this last from a shepherd's dog. Those different tribes of animals, however, though all of the same species, are of scarce any use to one another. The strength of the mastiff is not, in the least, supported either by the swiftness of the greyhound, or by the sagacity of the spaniel, or by the docility of the shepherd's dog. The effects of those different geniuses and talents, for want of the power or disposition to barter and exchange, cannot be brought into a common stock, and do not in the least contribute to the better accommodation and conveniency of the species. Each animal is still obliged to support and defend itself, separately and independently, and derives no sort of advantage from that variety of talents with which nature has distinguished its fellows. Among men, on the contrary, the most dissimilar geniuses are of use to one another; the different products of their respective talents, by the general disposition to truck, barter, and exchange, being brought, as it were, into a common stock, where every man may purchase whatever part of the product of other men's talents he has occasion for.

That the Division of Labour Is Limited by the Extent of the Market • As it is the power of exchanging that gives occasion to the division of labour, so the extent of this division must always be limited by the extent of that power, or, in other words, by the extent of the market. When the market is very small, no person can have any encouragement to dedicate himself entirely to one employment, for want of the power to exchange all that surplus part of the produce of his own labour, which is over and above his own consumption, for such parts of the produce of other men's labour as he has occasion for.

There are some sorts of industry, even of the lowest kind, which can be carried on nowhere but in a great town. A porter, for example, can find employment and subsistence in no other place. A village is by much too narrow a sphere for him; even an ordinary market town is scarce large enough to afford him constant occupation. In the lone houses and very small villages which are scattered about in so desert a country as the Highlands of Scotland, every farmer must be butcher, baker, and brewer for his own family ...

As, by means of water-carriage, a more extensive market is opened to every sort of industry than what land-carriage alone can afford it, so it is upon the seacoast, and along the banks of navigable rivers, that industry of every kind naturally begins to subdivide and improve itself; and it is, frequently, not till a long time after that those improvements extend themselves to the inland parts of the country. A broad-wheeled wagon, attended by two men, and drawn by eight horses, in about six weeks' time carries and brings back, between London and Edinburgh, near four tons' weight of goods. In about the same time, a ship, navigated by six or eight men, and sailing between the ports of London and Leith, frequently carries and brings back two hundred tons' weight of goods ... What goods could bear the expense of land-carriage between London and Calcutta? Or, if there were any so precious as to be able to support this expense, with what safety could they be transported through the territories of so many barbarous nations? Those two cities, however, at present carry on a very considerable commerce with each other, and, by mutually affording a market, give a good deal of encouragement to each other's industry.

Since such, therefore, are the advantages of water-carriage, it is natural that the first improvements of art and industry should be made where this conveniency opens the whole world for a market to the produce of every sort of labour, and that they should always be much later in extending themselves into the inland parts of the country. The inland parts of the country can, for a long time have no other market for the greater part of their goods but the country which lies round about them, and separates them from the sea coast, and the great navigable rivers. The extent of their market, therefore, must, for a long time, be in proportion to the riches and populousness of that country, and, consequently, their improvement must always be posterior to the improvement of that country. In our North American colonies, the plantations have constantly followed either the sea-coast or the banks of the navigable rivers, and have scarce anywhere extended themselves to any considerable distance from both. . . .

Of Restraints upon the Importation from Foreign Countries of Such Goods as Can Be Produced at Home • By restraining, either by high duties, or by absolute prohibitions, the importation of such goods from foreign countries as can be produced at home, the monopoly of the home market is more or less secured to the domestic industry employed in producing them. Thus the prohibition of importing either live cattle or salt provisions from foreign countries secures to the graziers of Great Britain the monopoly of the home market for butcher's meat. The high duties upon the importation of corn, which, in times of moderate plenty, amount to a prohibition, give a like advantage to the growers of that commodity. The prohibition of the importation of foreign woollens is equally favourable to the woollen manufactures. The silk manufacture, though altogether employed upon foreign materials, has lately obtained the same advantage. The linen manufacture has not yet obtained it, but is making great strides towards it. Many other sorts of manufacturers, have, in the same manner, obtained in Great Britain, either altogether or very nearly, a monopoly against their countrymen. The variety of goods, of which the importation into Great Britain is prohibited, either absolutely or under certain circumstances, greatly exceeds what can easily be suspected by those are [sic] not well acquainted with the laws of the Customs.

That this monopoly of the home market frequently gives great encouragement to that particular species of industry which enjoys it, and frequently turns towards that employment a greater share of both the labour and stock of the society than would otherwise have gone to it, cannot be doubted. But whether it tends either to increase the general industry of the society, or to give it the most advantageous direction, is not perhaps altogether so evident. . . .

To give the monopoly of the home market to the produce of domestic industry, in any particular art or manufacture, is in some measure to direct private people in what manner they ought to employ their capitals, and must, in almost all cases, be either a useless or a hurtful regulation. If the produce of domestic can be brought there as cheap as that of foreign industry, the regulation is evidently useless. If it cannot, it must generally be hurtful. It is the maxim of every prudent master of a family, never to attempt to make at home what it will cost him more to make than to buy. The tailor does not attempt to make his own shoes, but buys them of the shoemaker. The shoemaker does not attempt to make his own clothes, but employs a tailor. The farmer attempts to make neither the one nor the other, but employs those different artificers. All of them find it for their interest to employ their whole industry in a way in which they have some advantage over their neighbours, and to purchase with a part of its produce, or, what is the same thing, with the price of a part of it, whatever else they have occasion for.

What is prudence in the conduct of every private family, can scarce be folly in that of a great kingdom.

The general industry of the society never can exceed what the capital of the society can employ. As the number of workmen that can be kept in employment by any particular person must bear a certain proportion to his capital, so the number of those that can be continually employed by all the members of a great society must bear a certain proportion to the whole capital of that society, and never can exceed that proportion. No regulation of commerce can increase the quantity of industry in any society beyond what its capital can maintain. It can only divert a part of it into a direction into which it might not otherwise have gone;

and it is by no means certain that this artificial direction is likely to be more advantageous to the society than that into which it would have gone of its own accord.

Every individual is continually exerting himself to find out the most advantageous employment for whatever capital he can command. It is his own advantage, indeed, and not that of the society, which he has in view. But the study of his own advantage naturally, or rather necessarily, leads him to prefer that employment which is most advantageous to the society.

First, Every individual endeavours to employ his capital as near home as he can, and consequently as much as he can in the support of domestic industry; provided always that he can thereby obtain the ordinary, or not a great deal less than the ordinary, profits of stock.

Thus, upon equal, or nearly equal, profits, every wholesale merchant naturally prefers the home trade to the foreign trade of consumption, and the foreign trade of consumption to the carrying trade. . . . Upon equal, or only nearly equal, profits, therefore, every individual naturally inclines to employ his capital in the manner in which it is likely to afford the greatest support to domestic industry, and to give revenue and employment to the greatest number of people of his own country.

Secondly, Every individual who employs his capital in the support of domestic industry, necessarily endeavours so to direct that industry, that its produce may be of the greatest possible value.

The produce of industry is what it adds to the subject or materials upon which it is employed. In proportion as the value of this produce is great or small, so will likewise be the profits of the employer. But it is only for the sake of profit that any man employs a capital in the support of industry; and he will always, therefore, endeavour to employ it in the support of that industry of which the produce is likely to be of the greatest value, or to exchange for the greatest quantity either of money or of other goods.

But the annual revenue of every society is always precisely equal to the exchangeable value of the whole annual produce of its industry, or rather is precisely the same thing with that exchangeable value. As every individual, therefore, endeavours as much as he can both to employ his capital in the support of domestic industry, and so to direct that industry that its produce may be of the greatest value, every individual necessarily labours to render the annual revenue of the society as great as he can. He generally, indeed, neither intends to promote the public interest, nor knows how much he is promoting it. By preferring the support of domestic to that of foreign industry, he intends only his own security; and by directing that industry in such a manner as its produce may be of the greatest value, he intends only his own gain, and he is in this, as in many other cases, led by an invisible hand to promote an end which was no part of his intention. Nor is it always the worse for the society that it was no part of it. By pursuing his own interest he frequently promotes that of the society more effectually than when he really intends to promote it. I have never known much good done by those who affected to trade for the public good. It is an affectation, indeed not very common among merchants, and very few words need be employed in dissuading them from it.

What is the species of domestic industry which his capital can employ, and of which the produce is likely to be of the greatest value, every individual, it is evident, can, in his local situation, judge much better than any statesman or lawgiver can do for him. The statesman, who should attempt to direct private people in what manner they ought to employ their capitals, would not only load himself with a most unnecessary attention, but assume an authority which could safely be trusted, not only to no single person, but to no council or senate whatever, and which would nowhere be so dangerous as in the hands of a man who had folly and presumption enough to fancy himself fit to exercise it.

Aristocracy in a Democracy

ALEXIS DE TOCQUEVILLE

Democracy in America was published in 1835, when Alexis de Tocqueville, a French nobleman, was but 30 years of age. While agreeing with Smith that the "wealth of nations" is produced by freedom, he anticipates Marx in his concern for a new and especially harsh aristocracy which can emerge out of industrial democracy.

I HAVE SHOWN how democracy favors the growth of manufacturers and increases without limit the numbers of the manufacturing classes; we shall now see by what side road manufacturers may possibly, in their turn, bring men back to aristocracy.

It is acknowledged that when a workman is engaged every day upon the same details, the whole commodity is produced with greater ease, speed, and economy. It is likewise acknowledged that the cost of production of manufactured goods is diminished by the extent of the establishment in which they are made and by the amount of capital employed or of credit. These truths had long been imperfectly discerned, but in our time they have been demonstrated. They have been already applied to many very important kinds of manufactures, and the humblest will gradually be governed by them. I know of nothing in politics that deserves to fix the attention of the legislator more closely than these two new axioms of the science of manufactures.

When a workman is unceasingly and exclusively engaged in the fabrication of one thing, he ultimately does his work with singular dexterity; but at the same time he loses the general faculty of applying his mind to the direction of the work. He every day becomes more adroit and less industrious; so that it may be said of him that in proportion as the workman improves, the man is degraded. What can be expected of a man who has spent twenty years of his life in making heads for pins? And to

13

what can that mighty human intelligence which has so often stirred the world be applied in him except it be to investigate the best method of making pins' heads? When a workman has spent a considerable portion of his existence in this manner, his thoughts are forever set upon the object of his daily toil; his body has contracted certain fixed habits, which it can never shake off; in a word, he no longer belongs to himself, but to the calling that he has chosen. It is in vain that laws and manners have been at pains to level all the barriers round such a man and to open to him on every side a thousand different paths to fortune; a theory of manufactures more powerful than customs and laws binds him to a craft, and frequently to a spot, which he cannot leave; it assigns to him a certain place in society, beyond which he cannot go; in the midst of universal movement it has rendered him stationary.

In proportion as the principle of the division of labor is more extensively applied, the workman becomes more weak, more narrow-minded, and more dependent. The art advances, the artisan recedes. On the other hand, in proportion as it becomes more manifest that the productions of manufactures are by so much the cheaper and better as the manufacture is larger and the amount of capital employed more considerable, wealthy and educated men come forward to embark in manufactures, which were heretofore abandoned to poor or ignorant handicraftsmen. The magnitude of the efforts required and the importance of the results to be obtained attract them. Thus at the very time at which the science of manufactures lowers the class of workmen, it raises the class of masters.

While the workman concentrates his faculties more and more upon the study of a single detail, the master surveys an extensive whole, and the mind of the latter is enlarged in proportion as that of the former is narrowed. In a short time the one will require nothing but physical strength without intelligence; the other stands in need of science, and almost of genius, to ensure success. This man resembles more and more the administrator of a vast empire; that man, a brute.

The master and the workman have then here no similarity, and their differences increase every day. They are connected only like the two rings at the extremities of a long chain. Each of them fills the station which is made for him, and which he does not leave; the one is continually, closely, and necessarily dependent upon the other and seems as much born to obey as that other is to command. What is this but aristocracy?

As the conditions of men constituting the nation become more and more equal, the demand for manufactured commodities becomes more general and extensive, and the cheapness that places these objects within the reach of slender fortunes becomes a great element of success. Hence there are every day more men of great opulence and education who devote their wealth and knowledge to manufactures and who seek, by opening large establishments and by a strict division of labor, to meet the fresh demands which are made on all sides. Thus, in proportion as the mass of the nation turns to democracy, that particular class which is engaged in manufactures becomes more aristocratic. Men grow more alike in the one, more different in the other; and inequality increases in the less numerous class in the same ratio in which it decreases in the community. Hence it would appear, on searching to the bottom, that aristocracy should naturally spring out of the bosom of democracy.

But this kind of aristocracy by no means resembles those kinds which preceded it. It will be observed at once that, as it applies exclusively to manufactures and to some manufacturing callings, it is a monstrous exception in the general aspect of society. The small aristocratic societies that are formed by some manufacturers in the midst of the immense democracy of our age contain, like the great aristocratic societies of former ages, some men who are very opulent and a multitude who are wretchedly poor. The poor have few means of escaping from their condition and becoming rich, but the rich are constantly becoming poor, or they give up business when they have realized a fortune. Thus the elements of which the class of the poor is composed are fixed, but the elements of which the class of the rich is composed are not so. To tell the truth, though there are rich men, the class of rich men does not exist; for these rich individuals have no feelings or purposes, no traditions or hopes, in common; there are individuals, therefore, but no definite class.

Not only are the rich not compactly united among themselves, but there is no real bond between them and the poor. Their relative position is not a permanent one; they are constantly drawn together or separated by their interests. The workman is generally dependent on the master, but not on any particular master; these two men meet in the factory, but do not know each other elsewhere; and while they come into contact on one point, they stand very far apart on all others. The manufacturer asks nothing of the workman but his labor; the workman expects nothing from him but his wages. The one contracts no obligation to protect nor the other to defend, and they are not permanently connected either by habit or by duty. The aristocracy created by business rarely settles in the midst of the manufacturing population which it directs; the object is not to govern that population, but to use it. An aristocracy thus constituted can have no great hold upon those whom it employs, and even if it succeeds in retaining them at one moment, they escape the next; it knows not how to will, and it cannot act.

The territorial aristocracy of former ages was either bound by law, or thought itself bound by usage, to come to the relief of its serving-men and to relieve their distresses. But the manufacturing aristocracy of our age first impoverishes and debases the men who serve it and then abandons them to be supported by the charity of the public. This is a natural consequence of what has been said before. Between the workman and the master there are frequent relations, but no real association.

I am of the opinion, on the whole, that the manufacturing aristocracy which is growing up under our eyes is one of the harshest that ever existed in the world; but at the same time it is one of the most confined and least dangerous. Nevertheless, the friends of democracy should keep their eyes anxiously fixed in this direction; for if ever a permanent inequality of conditions and aristocracy again penetrates into the world, it may be predicted that this is the gate by which they will enter.

Controlling the Mischiefs of Faction

JAMES MADISON

*James Madison was one of three authors (all writing as Publius)
of the* Federalist Papers, *a collection of 85 papers published in
the New York press during late 1787 and early 1788. In the following, Paper Number 10, Madison argues that political order is
gained in essentially the same way as Smith's economic prosperity.
The only answer to freedom is more freedom.*

AMONG THE numerous advantages promised by a well constructed
Union, none deserves to be more accurately developed than its
tendency to break and control the violence of faction. The friend
of popular governments never finds himself so much alarmed for
their character and fate as when he contemplates their propensity to this dangerous vice. He will not fail, therefore, to set a due
value on any plan which, without violating the principles to
which he is attached, provides a proper cure for it. The instability,
injustice, and confusion introduced into the public councils have,
in truth, been the mortal diseases under which popular governments have everywhere perished, as they continue to be the
favorite and fruitful topics from which the adversaries to liberty
derive their most specious declamations. The valuable improvements made by the American constitutions on the popular models,
both ancient and modern, cannot certainly be too much admired;
but it would be an unwarrantable partiality to contend that they
have as effectually obviated the danger on this side, as was
wished and expected. Complaints are everywhere heard from our
most considerate and virtuous citizens, equally the friends of
public and private faith and of public and personal liberty, that
our governments are too unstable, that the public good is disregarded in the conflicts of rival parties, and that measures are too
often decided, not according to the rules of justice and the
rights of the minor party, but by the superior force of an inter-

ested and overbearing majority. However anxiously we may wish that these complaints had no foundation, the evidence of known facts will not permit us to deny that they are in some degree true. It will be found, indeed, on a candid review of our situation, that some of the distresses under which we labor have been erroneously charged on the operation of our governments; but it will be found, at the same time, that other causes will not alone account for many of our heaviest misfortunes; and, particularly, for that prevailing and increasing distrust of public engagements and alarm for private rights which are echoed from one end of the continent to the other. These must be chiefly, if not wholly, effects of the unsteadiness and injustice with which a factious spirit has tainted our public administrations.

By a faction I understand a number of citizens, whether amounting to a majority or minority of the whole, who are united and actuated by some common impulse of passion, or of interest, adverse to the rights of other citizens, or to the permanent and aggregate interests of the community.

There are two methods of curing the mischiefs of faction: the one by removing its causes; the other, by controlling its effects.

There are again two methods of removing the causes of faction: the one, by destroying the liberty, which is essential to its existence; the other, by giving to every citizen the same opinions, the same passions, and the same interests.

It could never be more truly said than of the first remedy that it was worse than the disease. Liberty is to faction what air is to fire, an ailment without which it instantly expires. But it could not be a less folly to abolish liberty, which is essential to political life, because it nourishes faction, than it would be to wish the annihilation of air, which is essential to animal life, because it imparts to fire its destructive agency.

The second expedient is as impracticable as the first would be unwise. As long as the reason of man continues fallible, and he is at liberty to exercise it, different opinions will be formed. As long as the connection subsists between his reason and his self-love, his opinions and his passions will have a reciprocal influence on each other; and the former will be objects to which the latter will attach themselves. The diversity in the faculties of men, from which the rights of property originate, is not less an insuperable obstacle to a uniformity of interests. The protection of these faculties is the first object of government. From the protection of different and unequal faculties of acquiring property, the possession of different degrees and kinds of property immediately results; and from the influence of these on the sentiments and views of the respective proprietors ensues a division of the society into different interests and parties.

The latent causes of faction are thus sown in the nature of man; and we see them everywhere brought into different degrees of activity, according to the different circumstances of civil society. A zeal for different opinions concerning religion, concerning government, and many other points, as well of speculation as of practice; an attachment to different leaders ambitiously contending for pre-eminence and power; or to persons of other descriptions, whose fortunes have been interesting to the human passions, have, in turn, divided mankind into parties, inflamed them with mutual animosity, and rendered them much more disposed to vex and oppress each other than to cooperate for their common good. So strong is this propensity of mankind to fall into mutual animosities that where no substantial occasion presents itself the most frivolous and fanciful distinctions have been sufficient to kindle their unfriendly passions and excite their most violent conflicts. But the most common and durable source of factions has been the various and unequal distribution of property. Those who hold and those who are without property have ever formed distinct interests in society. Those who are creditors, and those who are debtors, fall under a like discrimination. A landed interest, a manufacturing interest, a mercantile interest, a moneyed interest, with many lesser interests, grow up of necessity in civilized nations, and divide them into different classes, actuated by different sentiments and views. The regulation of these various and interfering interests forms the principal task of modern legislation and involves the spirit of party and faction in the necessary and ordinary operations of the government.

No man is allowed to be a judge in his own cause, because his interest would certainly bias his judgment, and, not improbably, corrupt his integrity. With equal, nay with greater reason, a body of men are unfit to be both judges and parties at the same time; yet what are many of the most important acts of legislation but so many judicial determinations, not indeed concerning the rights of single persons, but concerning the rights of large bodies of citizens? And what are the different classes of legislators but advocates and parties to the causes which they determine? Is a law proposed concerning private debts? It is a question to which the creditors are parties on one side and the debtors on the other. Justice ought to hold the balance between them. Yet the parties are, and must be, themselves the judges; and the most numerous party, or in other words, the most powerful faction must be expected to prevail. Shall domestic manufactures be encouraged, and in what degree, by restrictions on foreign manufactures, are questions which would be differently decided by the landed and the manufacturing classes, and probably by neither with a sole regard to justice and the public good. The apportionment of taxes on the various descriptions of property is an act which seems to require the most exact impartiality; yet there is, perhaps, no legislative act in which greater opportunity and temptation are given to a predominant party to trample on the rules of justice. Every shilling with which they overburden the inferior number is a shilling saved to their own pockets.

It is in vain to say that enlightened statesmen will be able to adjust these clashing interests and render them all subservient to the public good. Enlightened statesmen will not always be at the helm. Nor, in many cases, can such an adjustment be made at all without taking into view indirect and remote considerations, which will rarely prevail over the immediate interest which one party may find in disregarding the rights of another or the good of the whole.

The inference to which we are brought is that the *causes* of faction cannot be removed and that relief is only to be sought in the means of controlling its *effects*.

If a faction consists of less than a majority, relief is supplied by the republican principle, which enables the majority to defeat its sinister views by regular vote. It may clog the administration, it may convulse the society; but it will be unable to execute and mask its violence under the forms of the Constitution. When a majority is included in a faction, the form of popular government, on the other hand, enables it to sacrifice to its ruling passion or interest both the public good and the rights of other citizens. To secure the public good and private rights against the danger of such a faction, and at the same time to preserve the spirit and the form of populace government, is then the great object to which our inquiries are directed. Let me add that it is the great desideratum by which this form of government can be rescued from the opprobrium under which it has so long labored and be recommended to the esteem and adoption of mankind.

By what means is this object attainable? Evidently by one of two only. Either the existence of the same passion or interest in a majority at the same time must be prevented, or the majority, having such coexistent passion or interest, must be rendered, by their number and local situation, unable to concert and carry into effect schemes of oppression. If the impulse and the opportunity be suffered to coincide, we well know that neither moral nor religious motives can be relied on as an adequate control. They are not found to be such on the injustice and violence of individuals, and lose their efficacy in proportion to the number combined together, that is, in proportion as their efficacy becomes needful.

From this view of the subject it may be concluded that a pure democracy, by which I mean a society consisting of a small number of citizens, who assemble and administer the government in person, can admit of no cure for the mischiefs of faction. A common passion or interest will, in almost every case, be felt by a majority of the whole; a communication and concert result from the form of government itself; and there is nothing to check the inducements to sacrifice the weaker party or an obnoxious individual. Hence it is that such democracies have ever been spectacles of turbulence and contention; have ever been found incompatible with personal security or the rights of property; and have in general been as short in their lives as they have been violent in their deaths. Theoretic politicians, who have patronized this species of government, have erroneously supposed that by reducing mankind to a perfect equality in their political rights, they would at the same time be perfectly equalized and assimilated in their possessions, their opinions, and their passions.

A republic, by which I mean a government in which the scheme of representation takes place, opens a different prospect and promises the cure for which we are seeking. Let us examine the points in which it varies from pure democracy, and we shall comprehend both the nature of the cure and the efficacy which it must derive from the Union.

The two great points of difference between a democracy and a republic are: first, the delegation of the government, in the latter, to a small number of citizens elected by the rest; secondly, the greater number of citizens and great sphere of country over which the latter may be extended.

The effect of the first difference is, on the one hand, to refine and enlarge the public views by passing them through the medium of a chosen body of citizens, whose wisdom may best discern the true interest of their country and whose patriotism and love of justice will be least likely to sacrifice it to temporary or partial considerations. Under such a regulation it may well happen that the public voice, pronounced by the representatives of the people, will be more consonant to the public good than if pronounced by the people themselves, convened for the purpose. On the other hand, the effect may be inverted. Men of facetious tempers, of local prejudices, or of sinister designs, may, by intrigue, by corruption, or by other means, first obtain the suffrages, and then betray the interests of the people. The question resulting is, whether small or extensive republics are most favorable to the election of proper guardians of the public weal; and it is clearly decided in favor of the latter by two obvious considerations.

In the first place it is to be remarked that however small the republic may be the representatives must be raised to a certain number in order to guard against the cabals of a few; and that however large it may be they must be limited to a certain number in order to guard against the confusion of a multitude.

Hence, the number of representatives in the two cases not being in proportion to that of the two constituents, and being proportionally greatest in the small republic, it follows that if the proportion of fit characters be not less in the large than in the small republic, the former will present a greater option, and consequently a greater probability of a fit choice.

In the next place, as each representative will be chosen by a greater number of citizens in the large than in the small republic, it will be more difficult for unworthy candidates to practise with success the vicious arts by which elections are too often carried; and the suffrages of the people being more free, will be more likely to center on men who possess the most attractive merit and the most diffusive and established characters.

It must be confessed that in this, as in most other cases, there is a mean, on both sides of which inconveniencies will be found to lie. By enlarging too much the number of electors, you render the representative too little acquainted with all their local circumstances and lesser interests; as by reducing it too much, you render him unduly attached to these, and too little fit to comprehend and pursue great and national objects. The federal Constitution forms a happy combination in this respect; the great and aggregate interests being referred to the national, the local and particular to the State legislatures.

The other point of difference is the greater number of citizens and extent of territory which may be brought within the compass of republican than of democratic government; and it is this circumstance principally which renders factious combinations less to be dreaded in the former than in the latter. The smaller the society, the fewer probably will be the distinct parties and interests composing it; the fewer the distinct parties and interests, the more frequently will a majority be found of the same party; and the smaller the number of individuals composing a majority, and the smaller the compass within which they are placed, the more easily will they concert and execute their plans of oppression. Extend the sphere and you take in a greater variety of parties and interests; you make it less probable that a majority of the whole will have a common motive to invade the rights of other citizens; or if such a common motive exists, it will be more difficult for all who feel it to discover their own strength and to act in unison with each other. Besides other impediments, it may be remarked that, where there is a consciousness of unjust or dishonorable purposes, communication is always checked by distrust in proportion to the number whose concurrence is necessary.

Hence, it clearly appears that the same advantage which a republic has over a democracy in controlling the effects of faction is enjoyed by a large over a small republic—is enjoyed by the Union over the States composing it. Does the advantage consist in the substitution of representatives whose enlightened views and virtuous sentiments render them superior to local prejudices and to schemes of injustice? It will not be denied that the representation of the Union will be most likely to possess these requisite endowments. Does it consist in the greater security afforded by a greater variety of parties, against the event of any one party being able to outnumber and oppress the rest? In an equal degree does the increased variety of parties comprised within the Union increase this security? Does it, in fine, consist in the greater obstacles opposed to the concert and accomplishment of the secret wishes of an unjust and interested majority? Here again the extent of the Union gives it the most palpable advantage.

The influence of factious leaders may kindle a flame within their particular States but will be unable to spread a general conflagration through the other States. A religious sect may degenerate into a political faction in a part of the Confederacy; but the variety of sects dispersed over the entire face of it must secure the national councils against any danger from that source. A rage for paper money, for an abolition of debts, for an equal division of property, or for any other improper or wicked project, will be less apt to pervade the whole body of the Union than a particular member of it, in the same proportion as such a malady is more likely to taint a particular county or district than an entire State.

In the extent and proper structure of the Union, therefore, we behold a republic remedy for the diseases most incident to republican government. And according to the degree of pleasure and pride we feel in being republicans ought to be our zeal in cherishing the spirit and supporting the character of federalists.

PUBLIUS

THE IRON LAW OF OLIGARCHY
AND THE DEMOCRATIC MOLD

The Iron Law of Oligarchy

ROBERT MICHELS

When many factions are formed in a free society, each may indeed
check the others. But what of the free individual? Robert Michels
pondered this in his Political Parties *(1911), as indicated in the*
short introductory passage below.

THE DEMOCRATIC external form which characterizes the life of
political parties may readily veil from superficial observers the
tendency towards aristocracy, or rather towards oligarchy, which
is inherent in all party organization. If we wish to obtain light
upon this tendency, the best field of observation is offered by the
intimate structure of the democratic parties, and, among these,
of the socialist and revolutionary labour party. In the conservative parties, except during elections, the tendency to oligarchy
manifests itself with that spontaneous vigour and clearness which
corresponds with the essentially oligarchical character of these
parties. But the parties which are subversive in their aims exhibit
the like phenomena no less markedly. The study of the oligarchical manifestations in party life is most valuable and most
decisive in its results when undertaken in relation to the revolutionary parties, for the reason that these parties, in respect of
origin and of programme, represent the negation of any such
tendency, and have actually come into existence out of opposition thereto. Thus the appearance of oligarchical phenomena in
the very bosom of the revolutionary parties is a conclusive proof
of the existence of immanent oligarchical tendencies in every
kind of human organization which strives for the attainment of
definite ends.

In theory, the principle of social and democratic parties is the struggle against oligarchy in all its forms. The question therefore arises how we are to explain the development in such parties of the very tendencies against which they have declared war. To furnish an unprejudiced analytical answer to this question constitutes an important part of the task the author has undertaken.

In the society of today, the state of dependence that results from the existing economic and social conditions renders an ideal democracy impossible. This must be admitted without reserve. But the further question ensues, whether, and if so how far, within the contemporary social order, among the elements which are endeavouring to overthrow that order and to replace it by a new one, there may exist in the germ energies tending to approximate towards ideal democracy, to find outlet in that direction, or at least work towards it as a necessary issue.

The Democratic Mold

DAVID B. TRUMAN

In 1951, David B. Truman, at Columbia University, identified the conflict between the individual and groups and parties throughout the United States. The essay below is from Chapter V of The Governmental Process.

TAKING FIRST the two national labor federations,[1] we find the clearest instances of "democratic" structural formalities. Both place the formal control of the groups in an assembly of delegates, primarily drawn from the international unions. A typical constitutional provision is the following: "The convention shall be the supreme authority of the Organization and except as otherwise provided in the Constitution, its decisions shall be by a majority vote." Membership in the annual assemblies is based upon rather elaborate systems of representation. In the CIO each international union is entitled to from two to ten members, in proportion to paid-up membership. On a roll-call vote, the internationals cast one vote for each paid-up member. The directly chartered locals and the Industrial Union Councils cast one vote each. The AFL arrangement is similar. Both organizations show the dominant position in the internationals in the federal structure, the CIO somewhat more sharply than the AFL if voting arrangements alone are considered.

The annual conventions themselves, at least formally, dispose of a considerable authority. They elect (usually re-elect) the respective presidents, secretary-treasurers, and vice presidents who make up the governing boards that operate between conventions, call the Executive Committee by the CIO and the Executive Council by the AFL. In addition they elect the members of the convention committees, in which the most important

1. [This was written before the consolidation of AFL and CIO. However, there is every reason to believe that the conditions—the forms and the realities—are even more clearly present today.—*Editor.*]

28

business is initially transacted; this selection, however, amounts to a formal ratifying action, since the president's recommendations for these committee posts are made in advance of the convening of the electoral body.

Such formal arrangements as these are clearly the product of the values and practices of representative democracy, whatever may be the actual operation. They imply broad participation in the affairs of the group, regular answerability to the rank and file by means of annual elections, and some measure of delegate control of the purse strings. The parallel is less clear in financial practice, as the almost hallowed practice of legislative appropriations is not followed. In both federations the governing boards authorize expenditures. Nevertheless, in both groups the taxes on individuals and units—the primary source of the groups' revenue—are fixed in the constitution, and, as is customary in such cases, auditors' reports are submitted to the annual conventions, though they are not challenged.

The peculiarities of financial control in these federations are in part the result of the conflict situations in which these groups have operated, particularly in their early years; these arrangements thus illustrate the molding effect of external circumstances on the organized expression of group values. Because these circumstances are often close to warfare, in which exact knowledge of the group's resources would be a tactical advantage to opponents, individual unions and the federations have been cautious about publicizing finances. The following observations by Philip Murray early in 1940 illustrate the problem as it applies to individual unions:

The United Mine Workers of America, of which I am vice president, is one of the older and well established unions. It has virtually every coal operator under contract. . . . Its position is recognized as invulnerable. As a result, every six months, the United Mine Workers makes public its financial accounts. The SWOC [Steel Workers' Organizing Committee, now the United Steelworkers of America] is a new union, still violently opposed by a minority of the steel employers. It does not give out a public financial statement because of the obvious reason that its enemies would distort its meaning and significance for the purpose of maligning and harassing the SWOC.

The limitations on "democratic" control of the purse strings are not peculiar to the labor federations, nor are they most sharply illustrated by these groups. In varying degrees they appear in almost all large modern associations. In this respect and for much the same reasons, as will be noted in the next section, such associations have adopted some of the forms of the modern business corporation, which has been characterized as "an arrangement by which many men have delivered contributions of capital into the hands of a centralized control." These practices are implicitly in conflict with some of the "democratic" forms, as others have noted. The exigencies of operation, the dominance of attitudes reflected in business control patterns, and other factors have given these groups the appearance of mixture of differing elements. It is almost possible to rank associations and other groups on the basis of the extent of adoption of "corporate" forms. Such is the pervasiveness of the "democratic" preferences in our society, of course, that even the corporation shows their influence, as the semiritual of the annual stockholders' meeting suggests.

Illustrative of an almost balanced mixture of these elements, and of the conflicts that it creates, is the American Medical Association. Like the labor federations, the AMA structure places formal control in an annual assembly, designated in this case the House of Delegates. The house is made up of approximately 175 members, all but a handful of whom are elected for a two-year term by the State societies, the number allotted to each State being proportional to its medical population. Reapportionment takes place every three years, and each State is guaranteed not less than one representative. The remaining delegates are drawn one each from the scientific sections of the society, the medical corps of the military services, and the United States Public Health Service.

The powers of election exercised by the House of Delegates are impressive on paper. It elects the AMA's president (one year term), president-elect, and vice president. Although it also elects the secretary, general manager, and treasurer, these normally receive repeated reelections for a considerable period of years. The house elects a speaker and vice speaker as its presiding officers, as well as the members of its standing committees. Finally, it elects for five-year terms the nine members of the board of trustees.

This nominal power of election is evidence of the strength in the organization and in the community of "democratic" interests. These are to be seen also in some of the rules of election procedure. A standing rule of the House of Delegates provides that "the solicitation of votes for office is not in keeping with the dignity of the Medical profession, nor in harmony with the spirit of this Association and ... such solicitation shall be considered a disqualification for election to any office in the gift of the Association." The rule is apparently observed largely in the breach, and, as will be noted later, its effect may be the reverse of its apparent intent. But the "democratic" expectations of the community that it embodies remind one of the myths surrounding the New England town meeting, or, even more appropriately, the Quaker meeting, since it is assumed that the House of Delegates can reach a consensus on competing candidates without any electioneering by the latter.

The tendency to follow corporation practice in the association is perhaps best illustrated by the board of trustees, which is charged with the powers conferred by law upon a corporate board of directors. The board exercises, without direct control from the House of Delegates, complete authority over the property and finances of the organization. Such vestiges of control of the purse strings as remain to the house are further limited by the participation of the trustees in its deliberations, though without vote. The extent of the trustees' discretion is highlighted, moreover, by the fact that no more than half the association's revenues is normally derived from dues, the remaining coming from investments and the profits of its publishing ventures.

The extent of the conflicting patterns in the AMA is not completely indicated by the control over finances. Nominations for many of the elective positions whose incumbents are nominally chosen by the House of Delegates are made by the officers. The treasurer falls into this category, as do the standing committees of the house, candidates for these positions being nominated either by the president or by the trustees. The purely appointive power in the hands of the officers is also impressive. The trustees appoint all members of the AMA staff, including the members of the important Bureau of Medical Economics, the Bureau of Legal Medicine and Legislation, the editor of the AMA publications, and the business manager. The speaker of the House of Delegates, who is ex-officio one of the trustees, has complete appointive control over the reference and special committees, in which the main business of the house is actually conducted. He has, moreover, almost unlimited discretion in assigning matters to the various committees. Finally, the deliberations of several of these bodies are influenced by the officers through ex-officio membership by members of the standing committees and the paid staff. Thus the reference committee on amendments to the Constitution and by-laws includes all five members of the powerful Judicial Council, "supreme court" of the AMA, whose members are elected for a five-year term on nomination by the president. The reference committee on legislation and public relations similarly includes the director of the Bureau of Legal Medicine and Legislation.

The conflicts of interest that inevitably intrude upon and occur within the association have become involved in these contradictory tendencies of the organization's structure. Resistance to changes in policy have been facilitated by the restraining character of the "corporate" tendencies, and the obvious inconsistencies between the two tendencies have permitted the critical and the rebellious to verbalize their efforts in terms of "democracy" against "oligarchy."

If associations in the field of business and industry are examined, clearer evidence appears, as might be expected, of the preponderance of "corporate" practices, though they are somewhat softened by tendencies that appear also to satisfy the claims of "democracy."

This situation is particularly well illustrated by the trade association. Although virtually all such groups hold one or more meetings at the membership each year, the effective as well as much of the legal power in the organization rests with the officers, boards of directors, and the paid staff. Where the general membership plays a contributing part in policy making, it does so largely through committees. The TNEC study says of the large meetings: "If they are not a manner of performing activity, they are a means by which programs of activity are implemented and fostered. . . ." [2] The elected officers and boards of directors are in a peculiarly strategic position in the setting of policy, since they exercise the formal authority of the group (especially when the association is incorporated, as more than half are). The influence of the officers is further enhanced by their relations with the staff and particularly the paid executive.

The key importance of the paid executive of a trade association has been suggested in forthright terms:

The selection having been made, the executive can, to no inconsiderable degree determine the direction and emphasis of the associations program; and the executive in some instances probably has been quite as much a factor in determining the character of the association's program of activity as the nature of the industry, the size of the membership, and other circumstances . . .

His freedom of action, however, is subject to control by the directors, whose influence is increased in a large number of instances by the fact that the executive holds his position only from year to year. Among or behind the directors, moreover, may stand a few large financial contributors whose preferences and recommendations will carry special weight. The TNEC survey found that nearly half of the national and regional trade associations in 1937-38 received 40 per cent or more of their income from their four largest contributors. This situation is due largely to the common practice of apportioning dues by some measure of size or volume of business. It is worth noting that, although size of financial contribution may be a clue to the actual lines of influence, the formal patterns usually conform to the "democratic" mold. Nearly 90 per cent of the trade associations surveyed by the TNEC indicated that their formal voting arrangements permitted only one vote per member regardless of

2. [U. S. Temporary National Economic Committee, *Trade Association Survey*, pp. 33–35 and 384. Succeeding passages on trade associations are also from this study.—*Editor.*]

size or amount of contribution. Only 14 per cent allotted votes on some other basis.

The same kind of pattern emerges from an examination of the national business organizations. In the case of the Chamber of Commerce of the United States nominal policy control rests in the annual national convention. Delegates to this meeting are apportioned among the organization members, the individual and the firm members having no direct voice. This body elects some two thirds of the members of the board of directors, which is the locus of effective control in the association. The board is supplemented, however, by a national council made up of one representative for each organization member, which formally assists in planning the convention and advises and takes part in nominating members of the board of directors. With nearly three thousand organization members in the chamber, this body is not materially more significant than the annual convention itself.

The position and functions of the board of directors of the Chamber of Commerce are clearly of the "corporate" type. This body, numbering about fifty, elects the president and other officers of the organization, designates an executive committee from among its own membership, and appoints the principal officials of the headquarters staff. In addition, the board of directors passes upon all applications for membership, screens proposals submitted for action by the annual convention, and maintains close control over the organization's finances.

The importance of the last-named function is enhanced by the circumstance that the formal sources of policy-making authority are not identical with, nor even representative of, the major sources of financial support. This situation is similar to that in the American Medical Association, but it is more striking. Not only does the chamber, like the AMA, derive a sizable income from its publishing ventures, but also, its income from dues is derived from two different classes of members. The organization members, upon which the representative system in the annual convention is based, supply a relatively small proportion of the chamber's annual income, probably a good deal less than 10 per cent. This situation is the result of a deliberate policy, for the chamber's leadership has felt for a good many years that contributions from individuals and firms provide a firmer financial base than do those from the constituent commercial associations, whose own financial positions are often weak and subject to wide fluctuation. The chamber has thus concentrated its promotional efforts on potential individual and firm members. Although these members must also belong to one of the organization members, they will perhaps display interests divergent from those of the organization members, since they are men and firms financially strong enough to pay dues to at least two associations. To the extent that they do hold different interests, such individual and associate members are more directly, though not formally, represented in the key policy-making units than the constituent associations, whose continued support is less necessary on financial grounds. Such financial structure makes the financial powers exercised by the board of directors of more than ordinary significance.

The Chamber of Commerce thus illustrates sharply the symptoms of "centralized control" characteristic of modern large-scale business organizations, though many features of its formal organization show the impress of the democratic mold. One further feature that conforms to the latter pattern is of particular interest —the referendum. This device is also included in the formal organization of a number of the State medical societies, though it is virtually a dead letter. It is a permissive device in the organization of the National Association of Manufacturers and some labor unions, but is rarely used in either. Its use by the Chamber of Commerce is comparatively active. Decision to hold a referendum on a policy issue is taken by the board of directors, which appoints a special committee to look into the issue and make recommendations. A ballot on the issue, together with the committee's findings and a statement of the arguments counter to those supporting the committee's proposals, is sent to the organization members, each of which has as many votes as it is entitled to in the annual convention. The usual response is a large majority in favor of the committee's suggestions. Whatever may be the functional significance of the device, its existence is a striking instance of the impact of widespread community practices and values upon a group's formal organization.

Turning to a final example, the National Association of Manufacturers, we find, not unexpectedly, the clearest case of concentrated control, both formal and actual. Even here, however, the influence of "democratic" demands is apparent. Like the associations previously described, the NAM holds its annual convention (called the Congress of American Industry). The policy-making functions of this body are limited, as is illustrated by the fact that its sessions, with few exceptions, are open to members and nonmembers alike. This limitation is further evidenced by the absence of any representative system for the annual convention. Presumably all of the membership—currently claimed at sixteen thousand—could participate directly in its deliberations. This body elects roughly two thirds of the members of the board of directors, which numbers approximately 150, the exact number varying according to the size of the underlying membership. The most direct connection of the association's members with policy formulation, however, is through roughly a dozen standing committees—appointed by the board of directors—which submit recommendations to the board and its policy committees. About four fifths of the elected board members are chosen by a form of geographic proportional representation, the remainder being elected at large by the membership as a whole.

Despite these arrangements, centralized control is rather explicitly provided for in the organization. The board of directors, which has "full authority to effectuate the purposes and policies of the association," exercises the most extensive powers. It elects the president of the organization, chooses its own chairman (by custom the past president), and appoints an executive committee of about two dozen, whose chairman is usually the past chairman of the board. It elects the other officers of the association, appoints the principal members of the paid staff, makes changes in the by-laws, exercises complete authority over the budget, and approves changes in the constitution before they are submitted to the membership.

The nonelected members of the board are the officers, serving ex-officio, and a dozen to sixteen appointees. Among the latter are representatives of the National Industrial Council, a satellite organization of manufacturers' associations whose exact relations with the NAM have never been entirely clear. (The parent group supplies staff and headquarters facilities, and the Chairman of the NAM board is chairman of the NIC. This off-shoot appears to have little or no influence on NAM policy, functioning largely as a channel for spreading the parent organization's views among manufacturers not directly numbered among NAM members.) The elected members of the NAM board are chosen from a slate presented by a nominating committee appointed by the president, who also appoints members of the board to the policy committees, which sift proposals coming to the board and the executive committee. . . .

Tendencies toward minority control are not confined to the political interest groups used here for illustration, nor are they peculiar to this type of group. Writers of the most diverse political views and using the most widely variant methods of observation have called attention to the existence in almost all groups of an active minority—identified by such condemnatory terms as "oligarchy" and "old guard" or such approving ones as "public spirited citizens" and "civic leaders." The late Lord Bryce put the situation in these words:

In all assemblies and groups and organized bodies of men, from a nation down to the committee of a club, direction and decisions rest in the hands of a small percentage, less and less in proportion to the larger and larger size of the body, till in a great population it becomes an infinitesimally small proportion of the whole number. This is and always has been true of all forms of government, though in different degrees.

It is unnecessary here to examine all the varied formulations of this proposition.

The Perpetuation of our Political Institutions

ABRAHAM LINCOLN

One of Lincoln's lesser known but most thoughtful essays on government was his speech before the Young Men's Lyceum of Springfield, Illinois, January 27, 1838. How fitting for one with such orthodox views toward law to become the instrument of their ultimate enforcement!

IN THE great journal of things happening under the sun, we, the American People, find our account running, under date of the nineteenth century of the Christian era. We find ourselves in the peaceful possession, of the fairest portion of the earth, as regards extent of territory, fertility of soil, and salubrity of climate. We find ourselves under the government of a system of political institutions, conducing more essentially to the ends of civil and religious liberty, than any of which the history of former times tells us. We, when mounting the stage of existence, found ourselves the legal inheritors of these fundamental blessings. We toiled not in the acquirement or establishment of them—they are a legacy bequeathed us, by a *once* hardy, brave, and patriotic, but *now* lamented and departed race of ancestors. Theirs was the task (and nobly they performed it) to possess themselves, and through themselves, us, of this goodly land; and to uprear upon its hills and its valleys, a political edifice of liberty and equal rights; 'tis ours only, to transmit these, the former, unprofaned by the foot of an invader; the latter, undecayed by the lapse of time and untorn by usurpation, to the latest generation that fate shall permit the world to know. This task gratitude to our fathers, justice to ourselves, duty to posterity, and love for our species in general, all imperatively required us faithfully to perform.

How then shall we perform it? At what point shall we expect the approach of danger? By what means shall we fortify against it? Shall we expect some transatlantic military giant, to step the ocean, and crush us at a blow? Never! All the armies of Europe, Asia and Africa combined, with all the treasure of the earth (our own excepted) in their military chest; with a Buonaparte for a commander, could not by force take a drink from the Ohio, or make a track on the Blue Ridge, in a trial of a thousand years.

At what point then is the approach of danger to be expected? I answer, if it ever reach us, it must spring up amongst us. It cannot come from abroad. If destruction be our lot, we must ourselves be its author and finisher. As a nation of freemen, we must live through all time, or die by suicide.

I hope I am over wary; but if I am not, there is, even now, something of ill-omen, amongst us. I mean the increasing disregard for law which pervades the country; the growing disposition to substitute the wild and furious passions, in lieu of the sober judgment of Courts; and the worse than savage mobs, for the executive ministers of justice. This disposition is awfully fearful in any community; and that it now exists in ours, though grating to our feelings to admit, it would be a violation of truth, and an insult to our intelligence, to deny. Accounts of outrages committed by mobs, form the everyday news of the times. They have pervaded the country, from New England to Louisiana; they are neither peculiar to the eternal snows of the former, nor the burning suns of the latter; they are not the creature of climate— neither are they confined to the slaveholding, or the non-slaveholding States. Alike, they spring up among the pleasure hunting masters of Southern slaves, and the order loving citizens of the land of steady habits. Whatever, then, their cause may be, it is common to the whole country.

It would be tedious, as well as useless, to recount the horrors of all of them. Those happening in the State of Mississippi, and at St. Louis, are, perhaps, the most dangerous in example and revolting to humanity. In the Mississippi case, they first commenced by hanging the regular gamblers; a set of men, certainly not following for a livelihood, a very useful, or very honest occupation; but one which, so far from being forbidden by the laws, was actually licensed by an act of the Legislature, passed but a single year before. Next, negroes, suspected of conspiring to raise an insurrection, were caught up and hanged in all parts of the State: then, white men, supposed to be leagued with the negroes; and finally, strangers, from neighboring States, going thither on business, were, in many instances, subjected to the same fate. Thus went on this process of hanging, from gamblers to negroes, from negroes to white citizens, and from these to strangers; till, dead men were seen literally dangling from the boughs of trees upon every road side; and in numbers almost sufficient, to rival the native Spanish moss of the country, as a drapery of the forest.

Turn, then, to that horror-striking scene at St. Louis. A single victim was only sacrificed there. His story is very short; and is, perhaps, the most highly tragic, of anything of its length, that has ever been witnessed in real life. A mulatto man, by the name of McIntosh, was seized in the street, dragged to the suburbs of the city, chained to a tree, and actually burned to death; and all within a single hour from the time he had been a freeman, attending to his own business, and at peace with the world.

Such are the effects of mob law; and such are the scenes, becoming more and more frequent in this land so lately famed for love of law and order; and the stories of which have even now grown too familiar, to attract any thing more than an idle remark.

But you are, perhaps, ready to ask, "What has this to do with the perpetuation of our political institutions?" I answer, it has much to do with it. Its direct consequences are, comparatively speaking, but a small evil; and much of its danger consists, in the proneness of our minds, to regard its direct as its only consequences. Abstractly considered, the hanging of the gamblers at Vicksburg was of but little consequence. They constitute a portion of population that is worse than useless in any community; and their death, if no pernicious example be set by it, is never matter of reasonable regret with anyone. If they were annually swept from the stage of existence by the plague or small pox, honest men would, perhaps, be much profited by the operation. Similar too, is the correct reasoning, in regard to the burning of the negro at St. Louis. He had forfeited his life, by the perpetration of an outrageous murder, upon one of the most worthy and respectable citizens of the city; and had he not died as he did, he must have died by the sentence of the law, in a very short time afterwards. As to him alone, it was as well the way it was, as it could otherwise have been. But the example in either case was fearful. When men take it in their heads today, to hang gamblers, or burn murderers, they should recollect, that, in the confusion usually attending such transactions, they will be as likely to hang or burn someone who is neither a gambler nor a murderer as one who is; and that, acting upon the example they set, the mob of tomorrow, may, and probably will, hang or burn some of them by the very same mistake. And not only so; the innocent, those who have ever set their faces against violations of law in every shape, alike with the guilty, fall victims to the ravages of mob law; and thus it goes on, step by step, till all the walls erected for the defence of the persons and property of individuals, are trodden down, and disregarded. But all this even, is not the full extent of the evil. By such examples, by instances of the perpetrators of such acts going unpunished, the lawless in spirit are encouraged to become lawless in practice; and having been used to no restraint, but dread of punishment, they thus become absolutely unrestrained. Having ever regarded Government as their deadliest bane, they make a jubilee of the suspension of its operations; and pray for nothing so much as its total annihilation. While, on the other hand, good men, men who love tranquility, who desire to abide by the laws, and enjoy their benefits, who would gladly spill their blood in the defence of their country; seeing their property destroyed; their families insulted, and their lives endangered; their persons injured; and seeing nothing in prospect that forebodes a change for the better; become tired of, and disgusted with, a Government that offers them no protection; and are not much averse to a change in which they imagine they have nothing to lose. Thus, then, by the operation of this mobocratic spirit, which all must admit is now abroad in the land, the strongest bulwark of any Government, and particularly of those constituted like ours, may effectually be broken down and destroyed—I mean the *attachment* of the People. Whenever this effect shall be produced among us, whenever the vicious portion of population shall be permitted to gather in bands of hundreds and thousands, and burn churches, ravage and rob provision-stores, throw printing presses into rivers, shoot editors, and hang and burn obnoxious persons at pleasure, and with impunity, depend on it, this Government cannot last. By such things, the feelings of the best citizens will become more or less alienated from it; and thus it will be left without friends, or with too few, and those few too weak, to make their friendship effectual. At such a time and under such circumstances, men of sufficient talent and ambition will not be wanting to seize the opportunity, strike the blow, and overturn that fair fabric which for the last half century has been the fondest hope of the lovers of freedom, throughout the world.

I know the American People are *much* attached to their Government; I know they would suffer *much* for its sake; I know they would endure evils long and patiently, before they would ever think of exchanging it for another. Yet, notwithstanding all this, if the laws be continually despised and disregarded, if their rights to be secure in their persons and property are held by no better tenure than the caprice of a mob, the alienation of their affections from the Government is the natural consequence; and to that, sooner or later, it must come.

Here then, is one point at which danger may be expected.

The question recurs, "how shall we fortify against it?" The answer is simple. Let every American, every lover of liberty, every well-wisher to his posterity, swear by the blood of the Revolution never to violate in the least particular the laws of the country; and never to tolerate their violation by others. As the patriots of seventy-six did to the support of the Declaration of Independence, so to the support of the Constitution and Laws, let every American pledge his life, his property, and his sacred honor; let every man remember that to violate the law is to trample on the blood of his father, and to tear the character of his own, and his children's liberty. Let reverence for the laws be breathed by every American mother to the lisping babe that prattles on her lap—let it be taught in schools, in seminaries, and in colleges; let it be written in Primers, spelling books, and in Almanacs; let it be preached from the pulpit, proclaimed in legislative halls, and enforced in courts of justice. And, in short, let it become the *political religion* of the nation; and let the old and the young, the rich and the poor, the grave and the gay, of all sexes and tongues, and colors and conditions, sacrifice unceasingly upon its altars.

While ever a state of feeling, such as this, shall universally, or even, very generally prevail throughout the nation, vain will be every effort, and fruitless every attempt, to subvert our national freedom.

When I so pressingly urge a strict observance of all the laws, let me not be understood as saying there are no bad laws, nor that grievances may not arise, for the redress of which, no legal provisions have been made. I mean to say no such thing. But I do mean to say that, although bad laws, if they exist, should be repealed as soon as possible, still while they continue in force, for the sake of example they should be religiously observed. So also in unprovided cases. If such arise, let proper legal provisions be made for them with the least possible delay; but, till then, let them, if not too intolerable, be borne with.

There is no grievance that is a fit object of redress by mob law. In any case that arises, as for instance, the promulgation of abolitionism, one of two positions is necessarily true; that is, the thing is right within itself, and therefore deserves the protection of all law and all good citizens; or, it is wrong, and therefore proper to be prohibited by legal enactments; and in neither case, is the interposition of mob law, either necessary, justifiable, or excusable. . . .

[Lincoln then observes that the spirit of our Revolution continues to create a man who seeks great distinction and "disdains a beaten path."—*Editor.*]

But this state of feeling *must fade, is fading, has faded,* with the circumstances that produced it.

I do not mean to say, that the scenes of the revolution *are now* or *ever will* be entirely forgotten; but that like everything else, they must fade upon the memory of the world, and grow more and more dim by the lapse of time. In history, we hope, they will be read of, and recounted, so long as the bible shall be read; but even granting that they will, their influence *cannot be* what it heretofore has been. Even then, they *cannot be* so universally known, nor so vividly felt, as they were by the generation just gone to rest. At the close of that struggle, nearly every adult male had been a participator in some of its scenes. The consequence was, that of those scenes, in the form of a husband, a father, a son or a brother, *a living history* was to be found in every family—a history bearing the indubitable testimonies of its own authenticity, in the limbs mangled, in the scars of wounds received, in the midst of the very scenes related—a history, too, that could be read and understood alike by all, the wise and the ignorant, the learned and the unlearned. But *those* histories are gone. They *can* be read no more forever. They *were* a fortress of strength; but, what invading foeman could *never do*, the silent artillery of time *has done;* the leveling of its walls. They are gone. They *were* a forest of giant oaks; but the all-resistless hurricane has swept over them, and left only, here and there, a lonely trunk, despoiled of its verdure, shorn of its foliage; unshading and unshaded, to murmur in a few more gentle breezes, and to combat with its mutilated limbs, a few more ruder storms, then to sink, and be no more.

They *were* the pillars of the temple of liberty; and now that they have crumbled away, that temple must fall, unless we, their descendants, supply their places with other pillars, hewn from the solid quarry of sober reason. Passion has helped us; but can do so no more. It will in future be our enemy. Reason, cold, calculating, unimpassioned reason, must furnish all the materials for our future support and defence. Let those materials be molded into *general intelligence, sound morality,* and, in particular, *a reverence for the constitution and laws:* and, that we improved to the last; that we remained free to the last; that we revered his name to the last; that, during his long sleep, we permitted no hostile foot to pass over or desecrate his resting place; shall be that which to learn the last trump shall awaken our WASHINGTON.

Upon these let the proud fabric of freedom rest, as the rock of its basis; and as truly as has been said of the only greater institution, *"the gates of hell shall not prevail against it."*

Letter from Birmingham Jail

MARTIN LUTHER KING, JR.

Martin Luther King, Jr., shows himself in this famous letter to be a child of Lincoln but not one of his disciples. Faced with bad laws, can one follow Lincoln to the letter? King also asks questions about representation and psychological impact that are more contemporary issues.

April 16, 1963

MY DEAR FELLOW CLERGYMEN:

While confined here in the Birmingham city jail, I came across your recent statement calling my present activities "unwise and untimely." Seldom do I pause to answer criticism of my work and ideas. If I sought to answer all the criticisms that cross my desk, my secretaries would have little time for anything other than such correspondence in the course of the day, and I would have no time for constructive work. But since I feel that you are men of genuine good will and that your criticisms are sincerely set forth, I want to try to answer your statement in what I hope will be patient and reasonable terms....

I think I should indicate why I am here in Birmingham....

The purpose of our direct-action program is to create a situation so crisis-packed that it will inevitably open the door to negotiation. I therefore concur with you in your call for negotiation. Too long has our beloved Southland been bogged down in a tragic effort to live in monologue rather than dialogue....

You deplore the demonstrations taking place in Birmingham. But your statement, I am sorry to say, fails to express a similar concern for the conditions that brought about the demonstrations. I am sure that none of you would want to rest content with the superficial kind of social analysis that deals merely with effects and does not grapple with underlying causes. It is unfortunate that demonstrations are taking place in Birmingham, but it is

45

even more unfortunate that the city's white power structure left the Negro community with no alternative. . . .

You may well ask: "Why direct action? Why sit-ins, marches and so forth? Isn't negotiation a better path?" You are quite right in calling for negotiation. Indeed, this is the very purpose of direct action. Nonviolent direct action seeks to create such a crisis and foster such a tension that a community which has constantly refused to negotiate is forced to confront the issue. It seeks so to dramatize the issue that it can no longer be ignored. My citing the creation of tension as part of the work of the nonviolent-resister may sound rather shocking. But I must confess that I am not afraid of the word "tension." I have earnestly opposed violent tension, but there is a type of constructive, nonviolent tension which is necessary for growth. Just as Socrates felt that it was necessary to create a tension in the mind so that individuals could rise from the bondage of myths and half-truths to the unfettered realm of creative analysis and objective appraisal, so must we see the need for nonviolent gadflies to create the kind of tension in society that will help men rise from the dark depths of prejudice and racism to the majestic heights of understanding and brotherhood.

We know through painful experience that freedom is never voluntarily given by the oppressor; it must be demanded by the oppressed. Frankly, I have yet to engage in a direct-action campaign that was "well timed" in the view of those who have not suffered unduly from the disease of segregation. For years now I have heard the word "Wait!" It rings in the ear of every Negro with piercing familiarity. This "Wait" has almost always meant "Never." We must come to see, with one of our distinguished jurists, that "justice too long delayed is justice denied."

We have waited for more than 340 years for our constitutional and God-given rights. The nations of Asia and Africa are moving with jetlike speed toward gaining political independence, but we still creep at horse-and-buggy pace toward gaining a cup of coffee at a lunch counter. Perhaps it is easy for those who have never felt the stinging darts of segregation to say, "Wait." But when you have seen vicious mobs lynch your mothers and fathers at will and drown your sisters and brothers at whim; when you have seen hate-filled policemen curse, kick and even kill your black brothers and sisters; when you see the vast majority of your twenty million Negro brothers smothering in an airtight cage of poverty in the midst of an affluent society; when you suddenly find your tongue twisted and your speech stammering as you seek to explain to your six-year-old daughter why she can't go to the public amusement park that has just been advertised on television, and see tears welling up in her eyes when she is told that Funtown is closed to colored children, and see ominous clouds of inferiority beginning to form in her little mental sky, and see her beginning to distort her personality by developing an unconscious bitterness toward white people; when you have to concoct an answer for a five-year-old son who is asking: "Daddy, why do white people treat colored people so mean?"; when you take a cross-country drive and find it necessary to sleep night after night in the uncomfortable corners of your automobile because no motel will accept you; when you are humiliated day in and day out by nagging signs reading "white" and "colored"; when your first name becomes "nigger," your middle name becomes "boy" (however old you are) and your last name becomes "John," and your wife and mother are never given the respected title "Mrs."; when you are harried by day and haunted by night by the fact that you are a Negro, living constantly at tiptoe stance, never quite knowing what to expect next, and are plagued with inner fears and outer resentments; when you are forever fighting a degenerating sense of "nobodiness"—then you will understand why we find it difficult to wait. There comes a time when the cup of endurance runs over, and men are no longer willing to be plunged into the abyss of despair.

You express a great deal of anxiety over our willingness to break laws. This is certainly a legitimate concern. Since we so diligently urge people to obey the Supreme Court's decision of 1954 outlawing segregation in the public schools, at first glance it may seem rather paradoxical for us consciously to break laws. One may well ask: "How can you advocate breaking some laws and obeying others?" The answer lies in the fact that there are two types of laws: just and unjust. I would be the first to advocate obeying just laws. One has not only a legal but a moral responsibility to obey just laws. Conversely, one has a moral responsibility to disobey unjust laws. I would agree with St. Augustine that "an unjust law is no law at all."

Now, what is the difference between the two? How does one determine whether a law is just or unjust? A just law is a man-made code that squares with the moral law or the law of God. An unjust law is a code that is out of harmony with the moral law. To put it in the terms of St. Thomas Aquinas: An unjust law is a human law that is not rooted in eternal law and natural law. Any law that uplifts human personality is just. Any law that degrades human personality is unjust. All segregation statutes are unjust because segregation distorts the soul and damages the personality. It gives the segregator a false sense of superiority and the segregated a false sense of inferiority. Segregation, to use the terminology of the Jewish philosopher Martin Buber, substitutes an "I–it" relationship for an "I–thou" relationship and ends up relegating persons to the status of things. Hence segregation is not only politically, economically and sociologically unsound, it is morally wrong and sinful. Paul Tillich has said that sin is separation. Is not segregation an existential expression of man's tragic separation, his awful estrangement, his terrible sinfulness? Thus it is that I can urge men to obey the 1954 decision of the Supreme Court, for it is morally right; and I can urge them to disobey segregation ordinances, for they are morally wrong.

Let us consider a more concrete example of just and unjust laws. An unjust law is a code that a numerical or power majority group compels a minority group to obey but does not make binding on itself. This is *difference* made legal. By the same token, a just law is a code that a majority compels a minority to follow and that it is willing to follow itself. This is *sameness* made legal.

Let me give another explanation. A law is unjust if it is inflicted on a minority that, as a result of being denied the right to vote, had no part in enacting or devising the law. Who can say that the legislature of Alabama which set up that state's segregation laws was democratically elected? Throughout Alabama all sorts of devious methods are used to prevent Negroes from becoming registered voters, and there are some counties in which, even though Negroes constitute a majority of the population, not a single Negro is registered. Can any law enacted under such circumstances be considered democratically structured?

Sometimes a law is just on its face and unjust in its application. For instance, I have been arrested on a charge of parading without a permit. Now, there is nothing wrong in having an ordinance which requires a permit for a parade. But such an ordinance becomes unjust when it is used to maintain segregation and to deny citizens the First-Amendment privilege of peaceful assembly and protest.

I hope you are able to see the distinction I am trying to point out. In no sense do I advocate evading or defying the law, as would the rabid segregationist. That would lead to anarchy. One who breaks an unjust law must do so openly, lovingly, and with a willingness to accept the penalty. I submit that an individual who breaks a law that conscience tells him is unjust, and who willingly accepts the penalty of imprisonment in order to arouse the conscience of the community over its injustice, is in reality expressing the highest respect for law.

Of course, there is nothing new about this kind of civil disobedience. It was evidenced sublimely in the refusal of Shadrach, Meshach and Abednego to obey the laws of Nebuchadnezzar, on the ground that a higher moral law was at stake. It was practiced superbly by the early Christians, who were willing to face hungry lions and the excruciating pain of chopping blocks rather than submit to certain unjust laws of the Roman Empire. To a degree, academic freedom is a reality today because Socrates practiced civil disobedience. In our own nation, the Boston Tea Party represented a massive act of civil disobedience.

We should never forget that everything Adolf Hitler did in Germany was "legal" and everything the Hungarian freedom fighters did in Hungary was "illegal." It was "illegal" to aid and comfort a Jew in Hitler's Germany. Even so, I am sure that, had I lived in Germany at the time, I would have aided and comforted my Jewish brothers. If today I lived in a Communist country where certain principles dear to the Christian faith are suppressed, I would openly advocate disobeying that country's antireligious laws.

I must make two honest confessions to you, my Christian and Jewish brothers. First, I must confess that over the past few years I have been gravely disappointed with the white moderate. I have almost reached the regrettable conclusion that the Negro's great stumbling block in his stride toward freedom is not the White Citizen's Counciler or the Ku Klux Klanner, but the white moderate, who is more devoted to "order" than to justice; who prefers a negative peace which is the absence of tension to a positive peace which is the presence of justice; who constantly says: "I agree with you in the goal you seek, but I cannot agree with your methods of direct action"; who paternalistically believes he can set the timetable for another man's freedom; who lives by a mythical concept of time and who constantly advises the Negro to wait for a "more convenient season." Shallow understanding from people of good will is more frustrating than absolute misunderstanding from people of ill will. Lukewarm acceptance is much more bewildering than outright rejection.

I had hoped that the white moderate would understand that law and order exist for the purpose of establishing justice and that when they fail in this purpose they become the dangerously structured dams that block the flow of social progress. I had hoped that the white moderate would understand that the present tension in the South is a necessary phase of the transition from an obnoxious negative peace, in which the Negro passively accepted his unjust plight, to a substantive and positive peace, in which all men will respect the dignity and worth of human personality. Actually, we who engage in nonviolent direct action are not the creators of tension. We merely bring to the surface the hidden tension that is already alive. We bring it out in the open, where it can be seen and dealt with. Like a boil that can never be cured so long as it is covered up but must be opened with all its ugliness to the natural medicines of air and light, injustice must be exposed, with all the tension its exposure creates, to the light of human conscience and the air of national opinion before it can be cured. . . .

You speak of our activity in Birmingham as extreme. At first I was rather disappointed that fellow clergymen would see my nonviolent efforts as those of an extremist. I began thinking about the fact that I stand in the middle of two opposing forces in the Negro community. One is a force of complacency, made up in part of Negroes, who, as a result of long years of oppression, are so drained of self-respect and a sense of "somebodiness" that they have adjusted to segregation; and in part of a few middle-class Negroes who, because of a degree of academic and economic security and because in some ways they profit by segregation, have become insensitive to the problems of the masses. The other force is one of bitterness and hatred, and it comes perilously close to advocating violence. It is expressed in the various black nationalist groups that are springing up across the nation, the largest and best-known being Elijah Muhammad's Muslim movement. Nourished by the Negro's frustration over the continued existence of racial discrimination, this movement is made up of people who have lost faith in America, who have absolutely repudiated Christianity, and who have concluded that the white man is an incorrigible "devil."

I have tried to stand between these two forces, saying that we need emulate neither the "do-nothingism" of the complacent nor the hatred and despair of the black nationalist. For there is the more excellent way of love and nonviolent protest. I am grateful to God that, through the influence of the Negro church, the way of nonviolence became an integral part of our struggle.

If this philosophy had not emerged, by now many streets of the South would, I am convinced, be flowing with blood. And I am further convinced that if our white brothers dismiss as "rabble-rousers" and "outside agitators" those of us who employ nonviolent direct action, and if they refuse to support our nonviolent efforts, millions of Negroes will, out of frustration and despair, seek solace and security in black-nationalist ideologies—a development that would inevitably lead to a frightening racial nightmare. . . .

Let me take note of my other major disappointment. I have been so greatly disappointed with the white church and its leadership. Of course, there are some notable exceptions. . . . But despite these, I must honestly reiterate that I have been disappointed with the church. I do not say this as one of those negative critics who can always find something wrong with the church. I say this as a minister of the gospel, who loves the church; who was nurtured in its bosom; who has been sustained by its spiritual blessings and who will remain true to it as long as the cord of life shall lengthen.

When I was suddenly catapulted into the leadership of the bus protest in Montgomery, Alabama, a few years ago, I felt we would be supported by the white church. I felt that the white ministers, priests and rabbis of the South would be among our strongest allies. Instead, some have been outright opponents, refusing to understand the freedom movement and misrepresenting its leaders; all too many others have been more cautious than courageous and have remained silent behind the anesthetizing security of stained-glass windows.

In spite of my shattered dreams, I came to Birmingham with the hope that the white religious leadership of this community would see the justice of our cause and, with deep moral concern, would serve as the channel through which our just grievances could reach the power structure. I had hoped that each of you would understand. But again I have been disappointed.

I have heard numerous southern religious leaders admonish their worshipers to comply with a desegregation decision because it is the law, but I have longed to hear white ministers declare: "Follow this decree because integration is morally right and because the Negro is your brother." In the midst of blatant injustices inflicted upon the Negro, I have watched white churchmen stand on the sideline and mouth pious irrelevancies and sanctimonious trivialities. In the midst of a mighty struggle to rid our nation of racial and economic injustice, I have heard many ministers say: "Those are social issues, with which the gospel has no real concern." And I have watched many churches commit themselves to a completely otherworldly religion which makes a strange, un-Biblical distinction between body and soul, between the sacred and the secular. . . .

There was a time when the church was very powerful—in the time when the early Christians rejoiced at being deemed worthy to suffer for what they believed. In those days the church was not merely a thermometer that recorded the ideas and principles of popular opinion; it was a thermostat that transformed the mores of society. Whenever the early Christians entered a town, the people in power became disturbed and immediately sought to convict the Christians for being "disturbers of the peace" and "outside agitators." But the Christians pressed on, in the conviction that they were "a colony of heaven," called to obey God rather than man. Small in number, they were big in commitment. They were too God-intoxicated to be "astronomically intimidated." By their effort and example they brought an end to such ancient evils as infanticide and gladiatorial contests.

Things are different now. So often the contemporary church is a weak, ineffectual voice with an uncertain sound. So often it is an archdefender of the status quo. Far from being disturbed by the presence of the church, the power structure of the average community is consoled by the church's silent—and often even vocal—sanction of things as they are. . . .

I hope the church as a whole will meet the challenge of this decisive hour. But even if the church does not come to the aid of justice, I have no despair about the future. I have no fear about the outcome of our struggle in Birmingham, even if our motives are at present misunderstood. We will reach the goal of freedom in Birmingham and all over the nation, because the goal of America is freedom. Abused and scorned though we may be, our destiny is tied up with America's destiny. Before the pilgrims landed at Plymouth, we were here. Before the pen of Jefferson etched the majestic words of the Declaration of Independence across the pages of history, we were here. For more than two centuries our forebears labored in this country without wages; they made cotton king; they built the homes of their masters while suffering gross injustice and shameful humiliation—and yet out of a bottomless vitality they continued to thrive and develop. If the inexpressible cruelties of slavery could not stop us, the opposition we now face will surely fail. We will win our freedom because the sacred heritage of our nation and the eternal will of God are embodied in our echoing demands. . . .

One day the South will recognize its real heroes. They will be the James Merediths, with the noble sense of purpose that enables them to face jeering and hostile mobs, and with the agonizing loneliness that characterizes the life of the pioneer. They will be old, oppressed, battered Negro women, symbolized in a seventy-two-year-old woman in Montgomery, Alabama, who rose up with a sense of dignity and with her people decided not to ride segregated buses, and who responded with ungrammatical profundity to one who inquired about her weariness: "My feets is tired, but my soul is at rest." They will be the young high school and college students, the young ministers of the gospel and a host of their elders, courageously and nonviolently sitting in at lunch counters and willingly going to jail for conscience' sake. One day the South will know that when these disinherited children of God sat down at lunch counters, they were in reality standing up for what is best in the American dream and for the most sacred values in our Judaeo-Christian heritage, thereby bringing our nation back to those great wells of democracy which were dug deep by the founding fathers in their formulation of the Constitution and the Declaration of Independence. . . .

> Yours for the cause of Peace and Brotherhood,
> Martin Luther King, Jr.

The Origins of Capitalism

MAX WEBER

*In this succinct statement Max Weber provides a comprehensive
definition of capitalism, its prerequisites, preconditions, and functions in society. Drawn from his* General Economic History, *published in English in 1927, this essay imparts a special understanding of the kind of public order capitalism tends to impose on
society.*

CAPITALISM IS PRESENT wherever the industrial provision of the
needs of a human group is carried out by the method of enterprise, irrespective of what need is involved. More specifically, a
rational capitalistic establishment is one with capital accounting,
that is, an establishment which determines its income-yielding
power by calculation according to the methods of modern book-
keeping and the striking of a balance. The device of the balance
was first insisted upon by the Dutch theorist Simon Stevin in
the year 1698.

It goes without saying that an individual economy may be
conducted along capitalistic lines to the most widely varying
extent; parts of the economic provision may be organized capitalistically and other parts on the handicraft or the manorial
pattern. Thus at a very early time the city of Genoa had a part
of its political needs, namely those for the prosecution of war,
provided in capitalistic fashion, through stock companies. In the
Roman empire, the supply of the population of the capital city

with grain was carried out by officials, who however for this purpose, besides control over their subalterns, had the right to command the services of transport organizations; thus the liturgical or forced contribution type of organization was combined with administration of public resources. Today, in contrast with the greater part of the past, our everyday needs are supplied capitalistically, our political needs however through compulsory contributions, that is, by the performance of political duties of citizenship such as the obligation to military service, jury duty, etc. A whole epoch can be designated as typically capitalistic only as the provision for wants is capitalistically organized to such a predominant degree that if we imagine this form of organization taken away the whole economic system must collapse.

While capitalism of various forms is met with in all periods of history, the provision of the everyday wants by capitalistic methods is characteristic of the Occident alone and even here has been the inevitable method only since the middle of the nineteenth century. Such capitalistic beginnings as are found in earlier centuries were merely anticipatory, and even the somewhat capitalistic establishments of the sixteenth century may be removed in thought from the economic life of the time without introducing any overwhelming change.

The most general presupposition for the existence of this present-day capitalism is that of rational capital accounting as the norm for all large industrial undertakings which are concerned with provision for everyday wants. Such accounting involves, again, first, the appropriation of all physical means of production—land, apparatus, machinery, tools, etc.—as disposable property of autonomous private industrial enterprises. This is a phenomenon known only to our time, when the army alone forms a universal exception to it. In the second place, it involves freedom of the market, that is, the absence of irrational limitations on trading in the market. Such limitations might be of a class character, if a certain mode of life were prescribed for a certain class or consumption were standardized along class lines, or if class monopoly existed, as for example if the townsman were not allowed to own an estate or the knight or peasant to carry on industry; in such cases neither a free labor market nor a commodity market exists. Third, capitalistic accounting pre-supposes rational technology, that is, one reduced to calculation to the largest possible degree, which implies mechanization. This applies to both production and commerce, the outlays for preparing as well as moving goods.

The fourth characteristic is that of calculable law. The capital-istic form of industrial organizations, if it is to operate rationally, must be able to depend upon calculable adjudication and ad-ministration. Neither in the age of the Greek city-state (polis) nor in the patrimonial state of Asia nor in western countries down to the Stuarts was this condition fulfilled. The royal "cheap justice" with its remissions by royal grace introduced continual disturbances into the calculations of economic life. The proposi-tion that the Bank of England was suited only to a republic, not to a monarchy, was related in this way to the conditions of the time. The fifth feature is free labor. Persons must be present who are not only legally in the position, but are also economically compelled, to sell their labor on the market without restriction. It is in contradiction to the essence of capitalism, and the devel-opment of capitalism is impossible if such a propertyless stratum is absent, a class compelled to sell its labor services to live; and it is likewise impossible if only unfree labor is at hand. Rational capitalistic calculation is possible only on the basis of free labor; only where in consequence of the existence of workers who in the formal sense voluntarily, but actually under the compulsion of the whip of hunger, offer themselves, the costs of products may be unambiguously determined by agreement in advance. The sixth and final condition is the commercialization of eco-nomic life. By this we mean the general use of commercial instruments to represent share rights in enterprise, and also in property ownership.

To sum up, it must be possible to conduct the provision for needs exclusively on the basis of market opportunities and the calculation of net income. The addition of this commercialization to the other characteristics of capitalism involves intensification of the significance of another factor not yet mentioned, namely speculation. Speculation reaches its full significance only from the moment when property takes on the form of negotiable paper.

COMMERCIALIZATION AND EXPANSION OF OWNERSHIP

Commercialization involves, in the first place, the appearance of paper representing shares in enterprise, and, in the second place, paper representing rights to income, especially in the form of state bonds and mortgage indebtedness. This development has taken place only in the modern western world. . . .

In modern economic life the issue of credit instruments is a means for the rational assembly of capital. Under this head belongs especially the stock company. This represents a culmination of two different lines of development. In the first place, share capital may be brought together for the purpose of anticipating revenues. The political authority wishes to secure command over a definite capital sum or to know upon what income it may reckon; hence it sells or leases its revenues to a stock company.

Another and economically more important form of association is that for the purpose of financing commercial enterprise—although the evolution toward the form of association most familiar today in the industrial field, the stock company, went forward very gradually from this beginning. Two types of such organizations are to be distinguished; first, large enterprises of an interregional character which exceeded the resources of a single commercial house, and second, interregional colonial undertakings.

For interregional enterprises which could not be financed by individual entrepreneurs, finance by groups was typical, especially in the operations of the cities in the fifteenth and sixteenth centuries. In part the cities themselves carried on interregional trade, but for economic history the other case is more important, in which the city went before the public and invited share participation in the commercial enterprise which it organized. This was done on a considerable scale. When the city appealed to the public, compulsion was exercised on the company thus formed to admit any citizen; hence the amount of share capital was unlimited. Frequently the capital first collected was insufficient and an additional contribution was demanded, where today the liability of the share holder is limited to his share.

The great colonization companies formed another preliminary stage in the development of the modern stock company. The most significant of these were the Dutch and English East India companies, which were not stock companies in the modern sense. On account of the jealousy of the citizens of the provinces of the country the Dutch East India Company raised its capital by distributing the shares among them, not permitting all the stock to be bought up by any single city. The government, that is the federation, participated in the administration, especially because it reserved the right to use the ships and cannon of the company for its own needs. Modern capital accounting was absent as was free transferability of shares, although relatively extensive dealings in the latter soon took place. It was these great successful companies which made the device of share capital generally known and popular; from them it was taken over by all the continental states of Europe. Stock companies created by the state, and granted privileges for the purpose, came to regulate the conditions of participation in business enterprise in general, while the state itself in supervisory capacity was involved in the most remote details of business activity. Not until the eighteenth century did the annual balance and inventory become established customs, and it required many terrible bankruptcies to force their acceptance.

Alongside the financing of state needs through stock companies stands direct financing by measures of the state itself. This begins with compulsory loans against a pledge of resources and the issue of certificates of indebtedness against anticipated revenues. The cities of the Middle Ages secured extraordinary income by bonds, pledging their fixed property and taxing power....

In the sixteenth and seventeenth centuries an additional force working for the rationalization of the financial operations of rulers appeared in the monopoly policy of the princes. In part they assumed commercial monopolies themselves and in part they granted monopolistic concessions, involving of course the payment of notable sums to the political authority. The policy was most extensively employed in England and was developed in an especially systematic manner by the Stuarts, and there also it first broke down, under the protests of Parliament. Each new industry and establishment of the Stuart period was for this purpose bound up with a royal concession and granted a monopoly. The king secured important revenues from the privileges, which provided him with the resources for his struggle against Parliament. But these industrial monopolies established for fiscal purpose broke down almost without exception after the triumph of Parliament. This in itself proves how incorrect it is to regard, as some writers have done, modern western capitalism as an outgrowth of the monopolistic policies of princes. . . .

SPECULATION, WHOLESALING, EXCHANGE

We have recognized as characteristics and prerequisites of capitalistic enterprise the following: appropriation of the physical means of production by the entrepreneur, freedom of the market, rational technology, rational law, free labor, and finally the commercialization of economic life. A further motif is speculation, which becomes important from the moment when property can be represented by freely negotiable paper. Its early development is marked by the great economic crises which it called forth. In the course of the eighteenth century the wholesaler becomes finally separated from the retailer and comes to constitute a definite branch of the merchant class, whereas the Hansards, for example, were not yet typically wholesalers. Wholesaler trade is significant, first, because it evolved new commercial forms. One of these is the auction, which is the means by which the importing wholesaler turns over his goods as quickly as possible and secures the means for making his payment abroad. . . .

Further development consists in the appearance of a buying commission man alongside the one who sells, the former buying abroad without sight of the goods. The oldest form of such trade was based on samples. It is true that selling at a distance existed before this development, "merchantable goods" being bought and sold which must come up to the traditionally established quality; whether they did so was decided by mercantile courts of arbitration. Sale by sample, however, is a specifically modern form of trading at a distance. It played a fundamental role in commerce in the latter part of the eighteenth and the nineteenth centuries, being displaced by standardization and the specification of grades, which makes it possible to do away with the sending of samples. The new practice requires that grades be definitely established. It was on the basis of trading by grades that speculation and exchange dealings in connection with commodities became possible in the eighteenth century.

The fair is a prior stage of the exchange. The two have this in common, that trading takes place between merchants only; the difference consists in the physical presence of the goods in the case of the fair, and also in the periodical repetition of the fair itself. An intermediate type between the exchange and the fair is the so-called "permanent fair." In all the great commercial centers there arose in the sixteenth to the eighteenth centuries establishments which bore the name of exchange or "bourse." However, exchange dealings in the strict sense did not yet take place in them since the majority of those who frequented them were not local persons but nonresident merchants who resorted to the "exchange" because of its connection with the fair and because the goods were typically on the spot or represented by samples and were dealt in on this basis and not according to standard grades. Exchange dealing in the modern sense first developed in the field of negotiable paper and money, not in that of goods, the former being standardized by nature. Only in the course of the nineteenth century were those commodities added which could be graded with sufficient accuracy.

The innovation in developed exchange dealings is the system of rational dealing in futures or speculation for a rise, i.e., selling with a view to buying the goods at a lower figure before the date of delivery. It could nowhere be systematically carried out as in a modern exchange, where speculation for a rise is always present in opposition to speculation for a fall. The first objects subject to futures trading were money, especially paper money and bank notes, state annuities, and colonial paper. Here there could be difference of opinion as to the effect of political occurrence or the yield of enterprise and hence these instruments were an appropriate object for the practice of speculation. In contrast, industrial paper is entirely absent from the earliest price current bulletins. Such speculation underwent an enormous expansion with the building of railroads; these provided the paper which first unchained the speculative urge. Under the head of goods, grains, and a few colonial products available in large volume, and then other goods, were drawn into the circle of exchange speculation during the nineteenth century.

For the development of a wholesale trade carried out in such fashion, and specifically for speculative trade, the indispensable prerequisite was the presence of an adequate news service and an adequate commercial organization. A public news service, such as forms the basis of exchange dealings today, developed quite late. In the eighteenth century, not only did the English Parliament keep its proceedings secret, but the exchanges, which regarded themselves as merchants' clubs, followed the same policy in regard to their news information. They feared that the publication of general prices would lead to ill feeling and might destroy their business. The newspaper as an institution came into the service of commerce at an astonishingly late date.

In the field of commercial organization nothing was changed, at least in principle, in the period before the introduction of the railroads.

The railway is the most revolutionary instrumentality known to history, for economic life in general and not merely for commerce, but the railway was dependent on the age of iron; and it also like so many other things, was the plaything of princely and courtier interests.

THE DEVELOPMENT OF INDUSTRIAL TECHNIQUE

It is not easy to define accurately the concept of the factory. We think at once of the steam engine and the mechanization of work, but the machine had its forerunner in what we call "apparatus"—labor appliances which had to be utilized in the same way as the machine but which as a rule were driven by water power. The distinction is that the apparatus works as the servant of the man while in modern machines the inverse relation holds.

The real distinguishing characteristic of the modern factory is in general, however, not the implements of work applied, but the concentration of ownership of work place, means of work, source of power and raw material in one and the same hand, that of the entrepreneur. This combination was only exceptionally met with before the eighteenth century.

Tracing the English development, which determined the character of the evolution of capitalism—although England followed the example of other countries such as Italy—we find the following stages: 1. The oldest real factory which can be identified (though it was still driven by water power) was a silk factory at Derwent, near Derby, in 1719. It was conducted on the basis of a patent, the owner of which had stolen the invention in Italy. In Italy there had long been silk manufacture with various property relations, but the product was destined for luxury requirements and belonged to an epoch which is not yet characteristic for modern capitalism, although it must be named here because the implements of work and all material and product belonged to an entrepreneur. 2. The establishment of wool manufacture (1738) on the basis of a patent after the invention of an apparatus for running a hundred bobbins at once by the aid of water power. 3. The development of half-linen production. 4. The systematic development of the pottery industry through experiments in Staffordshire. Earthen vessels were produced under a modern division of labor and the application of water power, and with the ownership of work place and implements by an entrepreneur. 5. The manufacture of paper, beginning with the eighteenth century, its permanent basis being the development of the modern use of documents and of the newspaper.

The decisive factor, however, in the triumph of the mechanization and rationalization of work was the fate of cotton manufacture. This industry was transplanted from the Continent to England in the seventeenth century and there immediately began a struggle against the old national industry established since the fifteenth century, namely, wool, a struggle as intense as that in which wool had previously been involved against linen. The power of the wool producers was so great that they secured restrictions and prohibitions on the production of half-linen, which was not restored until the Manchester Act of 1736. The factory production of cotton stuff was originally limited by the fact that, while the loom had been improved and enlarged, the spindle remained on the medieval level, so that the necessary quantity of spun material was not available. A succession of technical improvements in the spindle after 1769 reversed this relation and with the help of water power and mechanical aids great quantities of usable yarn could be provided while it was impossible to weave the same quantity with corresponding speed. The discrepancy was removed in 1785 through the construction of the power loom by Cartwright, one of the first inventors who combined technology with science and handled the problems of the former in terms of theoretical considerations.

But for all this revolution in the means of work the development might have stopped and modern capitalism in its most characteristic form never have appeared. Its victory was decided by coal and iron. We know that coal had been used in consumption, even in the Middle Ages, as in London, in Luttich and Zwickau. But until the eighteenth century the technique was determined by the fact that smelting and all preparation of iron was done with charcoal. The deforestation of England resulted, while Germany was saved from this fate by the circumstance that in the seventeenth and eighteenth centuries it was untouched by the capitalistic development. The solution of the problem was reached through the coking of coal, which was discovered in 1735, and the use of coke in blast furnace operation, which was undertaken in 1740. Another step in advance was made in 1784 when the puddling process was introduced as an innovation. The threat to mining was removed by the invention of the steam engine. Crude attempts first showed the possibility of lifting water with fire and between 1670 and 1770, and further toward the end of the eighteenth century, the steam engine arrived at the stage of serviceability which made it possible to produce the amount of coal necessary for modern industry.

The significance of the development just portrayed is to be found in three consequences. In the first place, coal and iron released technology and productive possibilities from the limitations of the qualities inherent in organic materials; from this time

forward industry was no longer dependent upon animal power
or plant growth. Through a process of exhaustive exploitation,
fossil fuel, and by its aid iron ore, were brought up to the light of
day, and by means of both men achieved the possibility of extending production to a degree which would have previously
been beyond bounds of the conceivable. Thus iron became the
most important factor in the development of capitalism; what
would have happened to this system or to Europe in the absence
of this development we do not know.

The second point is that the mechanization of the production
process through the steam engine liberated production from the
organic limitations of human labor. Not altogether, it is true, for
it goes without saying that labor was indispensable for the tending
of machines. But the mechanizing process has always and everywhere been introduced to the definite end of releasing labor;
every new invention signifies the extensive displacement of hand
workers by a relatively small manpower for machine supervision.

Finally, through the union with science, the production of
goods was emancipated from all the bonds of inherited tradition,
and came under the dominance of the freely roving intelligence.
It is true that most of the inventions of the eighteenth century
were not made in a scientific manner; when the coking process
was discovered no one suspected what its chemical significance
might be. The connection of industry with modern science, especially the systematic work of the laboratories, beginning with
Justus von Liebig,[1] enabled industry to become what it is today
and so brought capitalism to its full development.

The recruiting of the labor force for the new form of production, as it developed in England in the eighteenth century, resting upon the concentration of all the means of production in the
hands of the entrepreneur, was carried out by means of compulsion, though of an indirect sort. Under this head belong especially the Poor Law, and the Statute of Apprentices of Queen
Elizabeth. These measures had become necessary in consequence
of the large number of people wandering about the country who

1. [German chemist, 1803–73. In the 1820's he established a teaching
laboratory, particularly for analyses in organic chemistry, making many important contributions and training many leading chemists.—*Editor.*]

had been rendered destitute by the revolution in the agricultural system. Its displacement of the small dependent peasant by large renters and the transformation of arable land into sheep pastures —although the latter has occasionally been overestimated— worked together constantly to reduce the amount of labor force required on the land and to bring into being a surplus population, which was subjected to compulsory labor. Anyone who did not take a job voluntarily was thrust into the workhouse with its strict discipline; and anyone who left a position without a certificate from the master or entrepreneur was treated as a vagabond. No unemployed person was supported except under the compulsion of entering the workhouse.

In the market for the products of these newly established industries, two great sources of demand appeared, namely war and luxury, the military administration and court requirements. . . . [Weber goes on to discuss the importance of the great mercenary armies and their use of the iron and cotton industries, as well as the importance of court and nobility in encouraging and supporting many manufactures. However, all through the discussion he tends to reduce their importance as factors underlying capitalist developments, despite the views of Sombart and others. —Editor.]

The decisive impetus toward capitalism could come only from one source, namely a mass market demand, which again could arise only in a small proportion of the luxury industries through the democratization of the demand, especially along the line of production of substitutes for the luxury goods of the upper classes. This phenomenon is characterized by price competition, while the luxury industries working for the court follow the handicraft principle of competition in quality. The first example of the policy of a state organization entering upon price competition is afforded in England at the close of the fifteenth century, when the effort was made to undersell Flemish wool, an object which was promoted by numerous export prohibitions.

The great price revolution of the sixteenth and seventeenth centuries provided a powerful lever for the specifically capitalistic tendencies of seeking profit through cheapening production and lowering the price. This revolution is rightly ascribed to the continuous inflow of precious metals, in consequence of the great overseas discoveries. It lasted from the thirties of the sixteenth century down to the time of the Thirty Years' War, but affected different branches of economic life in quite different ways. In the case of agricultural products an almost universal rise in price set in, making it possible for them to go over to production for the market. It was quite otherwise with the course of prices for industrial products. By and large these remained stable or rose in price relatively little, thus really falling, in comparison with the agricultural products. This relative decline was made possible only through a shift in technology and economics, and exerted a pressure in the direction of increasing profit by repeated cheapening of production. Thus the development did not follow the order that capitalism set in first and the decline in prices followed, but the reverse; first the prices fell relatively and then came capitalism.

The tendency toward rationalizing technology and economic relations with a view to reducing prices in relation to costs, generated in the seventeenth century a feverish pursuit of invention. All the inventors of the period are dominated by the object of cheapening production; the notion of perpetual motion as a source of energy is only one of many objectives by this quite universal movement. The inventor as a type goes back much farther. But if one scrutinizes the devices of the greatest inventor of precapitalistic times, Leonardo da Vinci—for experimentation originated in the field of art and not that of science—one observes that his urge was not that of cheapening production but the rational mastery of technical problems as such. The inventors of the precapitalistic age worked empirically; their inventions had more or less the character of accidents. An exception is mining, and in consequence it is the problems of mining in connection with which deliberate technical progress took place.

A positive innovation in connection with invention is the first rational patent law, the English law of 1623, which contains all the essential provisions of a modern statute. Down to that time the exploitation of inventions had been arranged through a special grant in consideration of a payment; in contrast the law of 1623 limits the protection of the invention to fourteen years and makes its subsequent utilization by an entrepreneur conditional upon an adequate royalty for the original inventor. Without the stimulus of this patent law the inventions crucial for the development of capitalism in the field of textile industry in the eighteenth century would not have been possible.

Drawing together once more the distinguishing characteristics of western capitalism and its causes, we find the following factors. First, this institution alone produced a rational organization of labor, which nowhere previously existed. Everywhere and always there has been trade; it can be traced back into the stone age. Likewise we find in the most varied epochs and cultures war finance, state contributions, tax farming, farming of offices, etc., but not a rational organization of labor. Furthermore we find everywhere else a primitive, strictly integrated internal economy such that there is no question of any freedom of economic action between members of the same tribe or clan, associated with absolute freedom of trade externally. Internal and external ethics are distinguished, and in connection with the latter there is complete ruthlessness in financial procedure; nothing can be more rigidly prescribed than the clan economy of China or the caste economy of India, and on the other hand nothing so unscrupulous as the conduct of the Hindu foreign trader. In contrast with this, the second characteristic of western capitalism is a lifting of the barrier between the internal economy and external economy, between internal and external ethics, and the entry of the commercial principle into the internal economy, with the organization of labor on this basis. Finally, the disintegration of primitive economic fixity is also met with elsewhere, as for example in Babylon; but nowhere else do we find the entrepreneur organization of labor as it is known in the western world. . . .

If this development took place only in the Occident the reason is to be found in the special features of its general cultural evolution which are peculiar to it. Only the Occident knows the state in the modern sense, with a professional administration, specialized officialdom, and law based on the concept of citizenship. Beginnings of this institution in antiquity and in the Orient were never able to develop. Only the Occident knows rational law, made by jurists and rationally interpreted and applied, and only in the Occident is found the concept of citizen (*civis Romanus, citoyen, bourgeois*) because only in the Occident again are there cities in the specific sense. Furthermore, only the Occident possesses science in the present-day sense of the word. Theology, philosophy, reflection on the ultimate problems of life, were known to the Chinese and the Hindu, perhaps even of a depth unreached by the European; but a rational science and in connection with it a rational technology remained unknown to those civilizations. Finally, western civilization is further distinguished from every other by the presence of men with a rational ethic for the conduct of life. Magic and religion are found everywhere; but a religious basis for the ordering of life which consistently followed out must lead to explicit rationalism is again peculiar to western civilization alone.

Natural Harmony in a Freely Competitive Society

LUDWIG VON MISES

To Ludwig von Mises, the market is not merely a way of ordering economic man, as Smith, Weber and others would allow. Market economics is "praxeology," the science of society. This essay, from his massive Human Action *(1949), is representative of his view that the main trouble with capitalism is that it has never been tried.*

THE NATURAL SCARCITY of the means of sustenance forces every living being to look upon all other living beings as deadly foes in the struggle for survival, and generates pitiless biological competition. But with man these irreconcilable conflicts of interests disappear when, and as far as, the division of labor is substituted for economic autarky of individuals, families, tribes, and nations. Within the system of society there is no conflict of interests as long as the optimum size of population has not been reached. As long as the employment of additional hands results in a more than proportionate increase in the returns, harmony of interests is substituted for conflict. People are no longer rivals in the struggle for the allocation of portions out of a strictly limited supply. They become cooperators in striving after ends common to all of them. An increase in population figures does not curtail, but rather augments, the average shares of the individuals.

If men were to strive only after nourishment and sexual satisfaction, population would tend to increase beyond the optimum size to the limits drawn by the sustenance available. However, men want more than merely to live and to copulate; they want to live *humanly*. An improvement in conditions usually results, it is true, in an increase in population figures; but this increase lags behind the increase in bare sustenance. If it were otherwise, men would have never succeeded in the establishment of social bonds and in the development of civilization. As with rats, mice, and microbes, every increase in sustenance would have made population figures rise to the limits of bare sustenance; nothing would have been left for the seeking of other ends. The fundamental error implied in the iron law of wages was precisely the fact that it looked upon men—or at least upon the wage earners—as beings exclusively driven by animal impulses. Its champions failed to realize that man differs from the beasts as far as he aims also at specifically human ends, which one may call higher or more sublime ends.

The Malthusian law of population is one of the great achievements of thought. Together with the principle of the division of labor it provided the foundations for modern biology and for the theory of evolution; the importance of these two fundamental theorems for the sciences of human action is second only to the discovery of the regularity in the intertwinement and sequence of market phenomena and their inevitable determination by the market data. The objects raised against the Malthusian law as well as against the law of returns are vain and trivial. Both laws are indisputable. But the role to be assigned to them within the body of the sciences of human action is different from that which Malthus attributed to them.

Nonhuman beings are entirely subject to the operation of the biological law described by Malthus. For them the statement that their numbers tend to encroach upon the means of subsistence and that the supernumerary specimens are weeded out by want of sustenance is valid without any exception. With reference to the nonhuman animals the notion of minimum sustenance has an unequivocal, uniquely determined sense. But the case is different with man. Man integrates the satisfaction of the purely zoological impulses, common to all animals, into a scale of values, in which a place is also assigned to specifically human ends. Acting man also rationalizes the satisfaction of his sexual appetites. Their satisfaction is the outcome of a weighing of pros and cons. Man does not blindly submit to a sexual stimulation like a bull; he refrains from copulation if he deems the costs—the anticipated disadvantages—too high. In this sense we may, without any valuation or ethical connotation, apply the term *moral restraint* employed by Malthus.

Rationalization of sexual intercourse already involves the rationalization of proliferation. Then later further methods of rationalizing the increase of progeny were adopted which were independent of abstention from copulation. People resorted to the egregious and repulsive practices of exposing or killing infants and of abortion. Finally they learned to perform the sexual act in such a way that no pregnancy results. In the last two hundred years the technique of contraceptive devices has been perfected and the frequency of their employment increased considerably. Yet the procedures had long been known and practiced.

The affluence that modern capitalism bestows upon the broad masses of the capitalist countries and the improvement in hygienic conditions and therapeutical and prophylactic methods brought about by capitalism have considerably reduced mortality, especially infant mortality, and prolonged the average duration of life. Today in these countries the restriction in generating offspring can succeed only if it is more drastic than in earlier ages. The transition to capitalism—i.e., the removal of the obstacles which in former days had fettered the functioning of private initiative and enterprise—has consequently deeply influenced sexual customs. It is not the practice of birth control that is new, but merely the fact that it is more frequently resorted to. Especially new is the fact that the practice is no longer limited to the upper strata of the population, but is common to the whole population. For it is one of the most important social effects of capitalism that it deproletarianizes all strata of society. It raises the standard of living of the masses of the manual workers to such a height that they too turn into "bourgeois" and think and act like well-to-do burghers. Eager to preserve their standard of living for themselves and for their children, they embark upon birth control. With the spread and progress of capitalism, birth control becomes a universal practice. The transition to capitalism is thus accompanied by two phenomena: a decline both in fertility rates and in mortality rates. The average duration of life is prolonged.

In the days of Malthus it was not yet possible to observe these demographical characteristics of capitalism. Today it is no longer permissible to question them. But, blinded by romantic prepossessions, many describe them as phenomena of decline and degeneration peculiar only to the white-skinned peoples of Western civilization, grown old and decrepit. These romantics are seriously alarmed by the fact that the Asiatics do not practice birth control to the same extent to which it is practiced in Western Europe, North America, and Australia. As modern methods of fighting and preventing disease have brought about a drop in mortality rates with these Oriental peoples too, their population figures grow more rapidly than those of the Western nations. Will not the indigenes of India, Malaya, China, and Japan, who themselves did not contribute to the technological and therapeutical achievements of the West, but received them as an unexpected present, in the end by the sheer superiority of their numbers squeeze out the peoples of European descent?

These fears are groundless. Historical experience shows that all Caucasian peoples reacted to the drop in mortality figures brought about by capitalism with a drop in the birth rate. Of course, from such historical experience no general law may be deduced. But praxeological reflection demonstrates that there exists between these two phenomena a necessary concatenation. An improvement in the external conditions of well-being makes possible a corresponding increase in population figures. However, if the additional quantity of the means of sustenance is completely absorbed by rearing an additional number of people, nothing is left for a further improvement in the standard of living. The march of civilization is arrested; mankind reaches a state of stagnation.

The case becomes still more obvious if we assume that a prophylactic invention is made by a lucky chance and that its practical application requires neither a considerable investment of capital nor considerable current expenditure. Of course, modern medical research and still more its utilization absorb huge amounts of capital and labor. They are products of capitalism. They would never have come into existence in a noncapitalist environment. But there were, in earlier days, instances of a different character. The practice of smallpox inoculation did not originate from expensive laboratory research and, in its original crude form, could be applied at trifling costs. Now, what would the results of smallpox inoculation have been if its practice had become general in a precapitalist country not committed to birth control? It would have increased population figures without increasing sustenance, it would have impaired the average standard of living. It would not have been a blessing, but a curse.

Conditions in Asia and Africa are, by and large, the same. These backward peoples receive the devices for fighting and preventing disease ready-made from the West. It is true that in some of these countries imported foreign capital and the adoption of foreign technological methods by the comparatively small domestic capital synchronously tend to increase the per capita output of labor and thus to bring about a tendency toward an improvement in the average standard of living. However, this does not sufficiently counterbalance the opposite tendency resulting from the drop in mortality rates not accompanied by an adequate fall in fertility rates. The contact with the West has not yet benefited these peoples because it has not yet affected their minds; it has not freed them from age-old superstitions, prejudices, and misapprehensions; it has merely altered their technological and therapeutical knowledge.

The reformers of the Oriental peoples want to secure for their fellow citizens the material well-being that the Western nations enjoy. Deluded by Marxian, nationalist, and militarist ideas they think that all that is needed for the attainment of this end is the introduction of European and American technology. Neither the Slavonic Bolsheviks and nationalists nor their sympathizers in the Indies, in China, and in Japan realize that what their peoples need most is not Western technology, but the social order which in addition to other achievements has generated this technological knowledge. They lack first of all economic freedom and private initiative, entrepreneurs and capitalism. But they look only for engineers and machines. What separates East and West is the social and economic system. The East is foreign to the Western spirit that has created capitalism. It is of no use to import the paraphernalia of capitalism without admitting capitalism as such. No achievement of capitalist civilization would have been accomplished in a noncapitalistic environment or can be preserved in a world without a market economy. . . .

The peoples who have developed the system of the market economy and cling to it are in every respect superior to all other peoples. The fact that they are eager to preserve peace is not a mark of their weakness and inability to wage war. They love peace because they know that armed conflicts are pernicious and disintegrate the social division of labor. But if war becomes unavoidable, they show their superior efficiency in military affairs too. They repel the barbarian aggressors whatever their numbers may be.

The purposive adjustment of the birth rate to the supply of the material potentialities of well-being is an indispensable condition of human life and action, of civilization, and of any improvement in wealth and welfare. Whether the only beneficial method of birth control is abstention from coitus is a question which must be decided from the point of view of bodily and mental hygiene. It is absurd to confuse the issue by referring to ethical precepts developed in ages which were faced with different conditions. However, praxeology is not interested in the theological aspects of the problem. It has merely to establish the fact that where there is no limitation of offspring there cannot be any question of civilization and improvement in the standard of living.

A socialist commonwealth would be under the necessity of regulating the fertility rate by authoritarian control. It would have to regiment the sexual life of its wards no less than all other spheres of their conduct. In the market economy every individual is spontaneously intent upon not begetting children whom he could not rear without considerably lowering his family's standard of life. Thus the growth of population beyond the optimum size as determined by the supply of capital available and the state of technological knowledge is checked. The interests of each individual coincide with those of all other individuals. . . .

From time immemorial men have prattled about the blissful conditions their ancestors enjoyed in the original "state of nature." From old myths, fables, and poems the image of this primitive happiness passed into many popular philosophies of the seventeenth and eighteenth centuries. In their language the term *natural* denoted what was good and beneficial in human affairs, while the term *civilization* had the connotation of opprobrium. The fall of man was seen in the deviation from the primitive conditions of ages in which there was but little difference between man and other animals. At that time, these romantic eulogists of the past asserted, there were no conflicts between men. Peace was undisturbed in the Garden of Eden.

Yet nature does not generate peace and good will. The characteristic mark of the "state of nature" is irreconcilable conflict. Each specimen is the rival of all other specimens. The means of subsistence are scarce and do not grant survival to all. The conflicts can never disappear. If a band of men, united with the object of defeating rival bands, succeeds in annihilating its foes, new antagonisms arise among the victors over the distribution of the booty. The source of the conflicts is always the fact that each man's portion curtails the portions of all other men.

What makes friendly relations between human beings possible is the higher productivity of the division of labor. It removes the natural conflict of interests. For where there is division of labor, there is no longer question of the distribution of a supply not capable of enlargement. Thanks to the higher productivity of labor performed under the division of tasks, the supply of goods multiplies. A preeminent common interest, the preservation and further intensification of social cooperation, becomes paramount and obliterates all essential collisions. Catallactic[1] competition is substituted for biological competition. It makes for harmony of the interests of all members of society. The very condition from which the irreconcilable conflicts of biological competition arise —viz., the fact that all people by and large strive after the same things—is transformed into a factor making for harmony of interests. Because many people or even all people want bread,

1. [Catallactic refers to all market phenomena or with all human relationships that have to do with peaceful but competitive exchange of scarce resources. It is "economics," but it subsumes a wider range of social relations than most living economists would want to.—*Editor.*]

clothes, shoes, and cars, large-scale production of these goods becomes feasible and reduces the costs of production to such an extent that they are accessible at low prices. The fact that my fellow man wants to acquire shoes as I do, does not make it harder for me to get shoes, but easier. What enhances the price of shoes is the fact that nature does not provide a more ample supply of leather and other raw materials required, and that one must submit to the disutility of labor in order to transform these raw materials into shoes. The catallactic competition of those who, like me, are eager to have shoes makes shoes cheaper, not more expensive.

This is the meaning of the theorem of the harmony of the rightly understood interests of all members of the market society. When the classical economists made this statement, they were trying to stress two points: First, that everybody is interested in the preservation of the social division of labor, the system that multiplies the productivity of human efforts. Second, that in the market society consumers' demand ultimately directs all production activities. The fact that not all human wants can be satisfied is not due to inappropriate social institutions or to deficiencies of the system of the market economy. It is a natural condition of human life. The belief that nature bestows upon man inexhaustible riches and that misery is an outgrowth of man's failure to organize the good society is entirely fallacious. The "state of nature" which the reformers and utopians depicted as paradisiac was in fact a state of extreme poverty and distress. "Poverty," says Bentham, "is not the work of the laws, it is the primitive condition of the human race." Even those at the base of the social pyramid are much better off than they would have been in the absence of social cooperation. They too are benefited by the operation of the market economy and participate in the advantages of civilized society.

The nineteenth-century reformers did not drop the cherished fable of the original earthly paradise. Frederick Engels incorporated it in the Marxian account of mankind's social evolution. However, they no longer set up the bliss of the *aurea aetas* [golden age] as a pattern for social and economic reconstruction. They contrast the alleged depravity of capitalism with the ideal happiness man will enjoy in the socialist Elysium of the future. The socialist mode of production will abolish the fetters by means of which capitalism checks the development of the productive forces, and will increase the productivity of labor and wealth beyond all measure. The preservation of free enterprise and the private ownership of the means of production benefits exclusively the small minority of parasitic exploiters and harms the immense majority of working men. Hence there prevails within the frame of the market society an irreconcilable conflict between the interests of "capital" and those of "labor." This class struggle can disappear only when a fair system of social organization— either socialism or interventionism—is substituted for the manifestly unfair capitalist mode of production.

Such is the almost universally accepted social philosophy of our age. It was not created by Marx, although it owes its popularity mainly to the writings of Marx and the Marxians. It is today endorsed not only by the Marxians, but no less by most of those parties who emphatically declare their anti-Marxism and pay lip service to free enterprise. It is the official social philosophy of Roman Catholicism as well as of Anglo-Catholicism; it is supported by many eminent champions of the various Protestant denominations and of the Orthodox Oriental Church. It is an essential part of the teachings of Italian Fascism and of German Nazism and of all varieties of interventionist doctrines. It was the ideology of the Sozialpolitik of the Hohenzollerns in Germany and of the French royalists aiming at the restoration of the house of Bourbon-Orléans, of the New Deal of President Roosevelt, and of the nationalists of Asia and Latin America. The antagonisms between these parties and factions refer to accidental issues—such as religious dogma, constitutional institutions, foreign policy—and, first of all, to the characteristic features of the social system that is to be substituted for capitalism. But they all agree in the fundamental thesis that the very existence of the capitalist system harms the vital interests of the immense majority of workers, artisans, and small farmers, and they all ask in the name of social justice for the abolition of capitalism. . . .

The advocates of socialism could even go farther and say: "Granted that each individual will be worse off under socialism than even the poorest under capitalism. Yet we spurn the market economy in spite of the fact that it supplies everybody with more goods than socialism. We disapprove of capitalism on ethical grounds as an unfair and amoral system. We prefer socialism on grounds commonly called noneconomic and put up with the fact that it impairs everybody's material well-being." It cannot be denied that this haughty indifference with regard to material well-being is a privilege reserved to ivory-tower intellectuals, secluded from reality, and to ascetic anchorites. What made socialism popular with the immense majority of its supporters was, on the contrary, the illusion that it would supply them with more amenities than capitalism. But however this may be, it is obvious that this type of prosocialist argumentation cannot be touched by the liberal reasoning concerning the productivity of labor.

If no other objections could be raised to the socialist plans than that socialism will lower the standard of living of all or at least of the immense majority, it would be impossible for praxeology to pronounce a final judgment. Men would have to decide the issue between capitalism and socialism on the ground of judgments of value and of judgments of relevance. They would have to choose between the two systems as they choose between many other things. No objective standard could be discovered which would make it possible to settle the dispute in a manner which allows no contradiction and must be accepted by every sane individual. The freedom of each man's choice and discretion would not be annihilated by inexorable necessity. However, the true state of affairs is entirely different. Man is not in a position to choose between these two systems. Human cooperation under the system of the social division of labor is possible only in the market economy. Socialism is not a realizable system of society's economic organization because it lacks any method of economic calculation.

The establishment of this truth does not amount to a depreciation of the conclusiveness and the convincing power of the antisocialist argument derived from the impairment of productivity to be expected from socialism. The weight of this objection raised to the socialist plans is so overwhelming that no judicious man could hesitate to choose capitalism. Yet this would still be a choice between alternative systems of society's economic organization, preference given to one system as against another. However, such is not the alternative. Socialism cannot be realized because it is beyond human power to establish it as a social system. The choice is between capitalism and chaos. A man who chooses between drinking a glass of milk and a glass of a solution of potassium cyanide does not choose between two beverages; he chooses between life and death. A society that chooses between capitalism and socialism does not choose between two social systems; it chooses between social cooperation and the disintegration of society. Socialism is not an alternative to capitalism; it is an alternative to any system under which men can live as *human* beings. To stress this point is the task of economics as it is the task of biology and chemistry to teach that potassium cyanide is not a nutriment but a deadly poison.

The convincing power of the productivity argument is in fact so irresistible that the advocates of socialism were forced to abandon their old tactics and to resort to new methods. They are eager to divert attention from the productivity issue by throwing into relief the monopoly problem. All contemporary socialist manifestoes expatiate on monopoly power. Statesmen and professors try to outdo one another in depicting the evils of monopoly. Our age is called the age of monopoly capitalism. The foremost argument advanced today in favor of socialism is the reference to monopoly.

Now, it is true that the emergence of monopoly prices (not of monopoly as such without monopoly prices) creates a discrepancy between the interests of the monopolist and those of the consumers. The monopolist does not employ the monopolized good according to the wishes of the consumers. As far as there are monopoly prices, the interests of the monopolist take precedence over those of the public and the democracy of the market is restricted. With regard to monopoly prices there is not harmony, but conflict of interests.

It is possible to contest these statements with regard to the monopoly prices received in the sale of articles under patents and copyrights. One may argue that in the absence of patent and copyright legislation these books, compositions, and technological innovations would never have come into existence. The public pays monopoly prices for things they would not have enjoyed at all under the competitive prices. However, we may fairly disregard this issue. It has little to do with the great monopoly controversy of our day. When people deal with the evils of monopoly, they imply that there prevails within the unhampered market economy a general and inevitable tendency toward the substitution of monopoly prices for competitive prices. This is, they say, a characteristic mark of "mature" or "late" capitalism. Whatever conditions may have been in the earlier stages of capitalist evolution and whatever one may think about the validity of the classical economists' statements concerning the harmony of the rightly understood interests, today there is no longer any question of such a harmony.

As has been pointed out already, there is no such tendency toward monopolization. It is a fact that with many commodities in many countries monopoly prices prevail, and, moreover, some articles are sold at monopoly prices on the world market. However, almost all of these instances of monopoly prices are the outgrowth of government interference with business. They were not created by the interplay of the factors operating on a free market. They are not products of capitalism, but precisely of the endeavors to counteract the forces determining the height of the market prices. It is a distortion of fact to speak of monopoly capitalism. It would be more appropriate to speak of monopoly interventionism or of monopoly statism.

Those instances of monopoly prices which would appear also on a market not hampered and sabotaged by the interference of the various national governments and by conspiracies between groups of governments are of minor importance. They concern some raw materials the deposits of which are few and geographically concentrated, and local limited-space monopolies. However, it is a fact that in these cases monopoly prices can be realized even in the absence of government policies aiming directly or indirectly at their establishment. It is necessary to realize that consumers' sovereignty is not perfect and that there are limits to the operation of the democratic process of the market. There is in some exceptional and rare cases of minor importance even on a market not hampered and sabotaged by government interference an antagonism between the interests of the owners of factors of production and those of the rest of the people. However, the existence of such antagonisms by no means impairs the concord of the interests of all people with regard to the preservation of the market economy. The market economy is the only system of society's economic organization that can function and really has been functioning. Socialism is unrealizable because of its inability to develop a method for economic calculation. Interventionism must result in a state of affairs which, from the point of view of its advocates, is less desirable than the conditions of the unhampered market economy which it aims to alter. In addition, it liquidates itself as soon as it is pushed beyond a narrow field of application. Such being the case, the only social order that can preserve and further intensify the social division of labor is the market economy. All those who do not wish to disintegrate social cooperation and to return to the conditions of primitive barbarism are interested in the perpetuation of the market economy.

The Great Society and the Loss of Self-regulation

KARL MANNHEIM

Karl Mannheim offers an unusual rebuttal to the argument that capitalism is enough to produce prosperity and public order. It is possible, he says in Freedom, Power and Democratic Planning *(1950), that the very productivity of capitalist techniques, so well identified by von Mises, Weber, et. al., may have created profound weaknesses in the social fabric.*

MOST SYMPTOMS of maladjustment in modern society can be traced to the fact that a parochial world of small groups expanded into a great society in a comparatively short time. This unguided transformation caused manifold disturbances and unsolved problems throughout social life. They can be set right only with due attention to the circumstances surrounding the calamities.

Unguided, unplanned transition does not cause major disturbances where the social units are small and when sufficient time is allowed for adjustment by trial and error. Even then maladjustments occur through the occasional inexpediency of a prevailing pattern of action or thought in an unforeseen situation. Usually, however, a new adjustment is made with no hiatus in the process of socially coordinated living. The case is quite different when society develops on a large scale unguided. Here, too, innumerable efforts are made to replace obsolete patterns of behavior and organization by new ones; but either no new pattern can be found on the level of blind experimentation, or, if such a new solution emerges at last, there is a hiatus in which no satisfactory reaction is forthcoming. In such cases we shall speak of social disintegration.

While there is much talk of disintegration, the term is often

83

used too vaguely to convey any meaning. Surely we should not speak of disintegration if a social order cherished by the observer were to vanish and be replaced by another. This is social change indeed, but not social disintegration. The cardinal point is a gradual weakening of the prevailing social structure and of the forces that sustain it, without the simultaneous growth of a new order. It is true, there are borderline cases where we are uncertain whether the lack of a new solution is a symptom of transition only or whether a serious void threatens. But by and large we know the difference. Everyone knows that occasional unemployment of a few people is just a gap in adjustment, whereas recurrent unemployment, which in its cumulative effects upsets the working of a whole social order, should be considered a symptom of disintegration. The same applies to the moral sphere. People may occasionally be uncertain about what is right or wrong and this may be taken as a matter of course. But when mass anxieties prevail, because the general ideological upheaval leaves no sound basis for common action, and when people do not know where they stand or what they ought to think about the most elementary problems of life, then again we may rightly speak of the spiritual disintegration of society.

While we attempt to show in the following pages that we are living in such an age of disintegration, we of course do not mean that disintegration is ever total. Were this the case, we could no longer go on living. Even in a disintegrating society there are self-healing processes and spontaneous adjustments that make life somehow bearable. Still, even under conditions of comparative tranquillity, the sociologically trained eye can see the gaps in the social fabric, the void in the individual intellectual, moral, and emotional make-up. In a given situation, once the cumulative effects of disintegration get out of hand, implicit chaos becomes apparent to all. . . .

Uncontrolled growth in the economic system is . . . just one aspect of uncontrolled growth in modern society at large. Society is gradually becoming a conglomeration of smaller and larger groups, very often held together only by administrative agencies replacing the older small organic groups. By organic we mean that self-regulating power which is characteristic of small groups but gradually vanishes in large ones. There is nothing mysterious about this self-regulating power which guarantees a certain evenness, balance, and continuity in development so long as the size of the community is limited and everybody can see approximately how things will work out. There is no mystery about correlating supply and demand in a household economy where the decision about the goods to be produced and consumed is in the same hands. Nor is there mystery in correlating supply and demand when the craftsman works for a certain number of customers whom he knows personally and whose wishes he can foresee. There is even no special mystery about the self-regulating powers of the market as long as small units compete.

The phenomenon of self-regulation in small groups has been studied more extensively in the economic sphere, but the same self-regulation takes place in other spheres. Limited size allows everyone to understand what is required of him and what to expect from the group. In direct everyday contacts with other group members, each can discover for himself the causes of success or failure and seek collective remedies when things go wrong. The *Agora* of the Greek city, the market place of the medieval town, where the church, the guildhall, and the market stalls were close to one another, enabled the citizen to take in the whole orbit of his world at a glance. Differentiation of human activities and growth of the corresponding social types happened along the lines of gradually expanding cooperation. Everybody knew his function since he could clearly see how the village supplied the town and the town, the village; how the different occupations served and balanced each other and regulated their mutual relationships. Yet among the members not only were the formal relations of social hierarchy and function clearly defined but the whole edifice of growing society was still supported by the basic institutions of family, neighborhood, and community.

All this is not said in the spirit of eulogy. The narrow outlook, the inescapable limitations, would probably have made life in such a world unbearable for us. All we want to emphasize is the nature of an integrated social pattern which is now vanishing. The most adequate expression of this evanescence is the mushroom growth of the metropolis where the last traces of organic cohesion are fading away and the principle of common living, functional interdependence, and clarity of common purpose are completely destroyed.

Another important aspect of the same process is the disintegration of ancient forms of social control.

As long as the self-regulating powers of small groups remain undisturbed, action and thought are controlled by common sense and the rules fixed by custom and precedent. Traditions are ultimately the accumulated experience of successful adjustment. Acting on the basis of tradition has the advantage of saving the individual the trouble of making a choice, or of inventing new ways where the old are capable of solving the difficulty. But tradition and custom maintain their power to control events only so long as certain conditions prevail, and it is important to enumerate at least some of these. The tasks must be simple and recurrent, needing only limited organization for their performance. Only in these circumstances does the established pattern apply; as variety increases, tasks grow too complex. Rational analysis is necessary to divide the whole into its component parts, creating new combinations and transgressing precedents.

Tradition works only so long as transformation is slow and gradual and the home, the market, the church, and the city do not represent entirely different and even antagonistic influences; or if they do, there is time to reconcile these differences and to assimilate discordant habits. Thus, as long as growth is gradual, traditions will act as controls safeguarding the amount of conformity without which cooperation is impossible. You can act only if you can base your conduct upon reasonable expectation of how people will react. People can be united in war and peace only if certain basic values are tacitly accepted by the community. So long as the group is more or less homogeneous and people live in roughly the same sort of social and cultural surroundings, and so long as there is not too much rise and fall in the social scale, customary habits will remain stable.

Historically, not only have we passed from the stage of neighborhood community to the great society in a relatively short time, but this growth has frequently been by fits and starts. Technical development in itself undermined those conditions that were the mainstay of tradition. Whole groups were eradicated at times, as were the old English aristocracy in the Wars of the Roses or the rural workers during the Industrial Revolution; others were driven to emigrate by economic, political, or ecclesiastic forces.

This rapid, spasmodic transformation contributed to the disintegration of ancient group controls. We can scarcely maintain that we have been able to substitute adequately for them. Undoubtedly we have succeeded in inventing a few patterns of large-scale organization, like that of the army, the factory, the civil service. But none of these has developed the elasticity and responsiveness to human needs of the small group. We still take it for granted that large-scale organizations should be abstract, arbitrary, and dehumanizing, in emulation of the first great pattern of large-scale organization, the army. Today, after shattering experiences, we can see that the controls which prevail in the army and the factory have, in themselves, a demoralizing effect. In the long run treating men like the cogs and wheels of a machine can only lead to deliberate inefficiency or sabotage. The equation—natural controls in small groups, mechanical devices in large-scale organizations—no longer holds. For we know that the greatest demoralization of the individual arises from overformalization. The raw material for chaos is not the undisciplined barbarian but the overdisciplined factory worker or soldier who in consequence loses vitality whenever the plant closes down or when there is no one to give commands.

FAILURE OF LARGE-SCALE COORDINATION

As for special controls, an added irritant in modern society is the lack of successful coordination between different large-scale organizations. Developed as business enterprises, as state bureaucracies, or as voluntary associations, they frequently overlap in function. Uncoordinated institutions cancel each other's effectiveness. It was quite different in medieval society where, for example, the medieval guild was an elaborate system of well-defined functions, privileges, and prohibitions. Not only were the formal relationships between the members, their social hierarchy, and their functions within the community clearly established, not only were all aspects of their life, work, leisure, culture, and worship clearly shaped and determined by the purposes of the community, but the corporations themselves were coordinated. They constituted the medieval city and thus differed essentially from modern employers' associations or trade unions which have only segmental functions and are hardly controlled by the community. Admitting that a large-scale society cannot continue without a certain coordination of its institutions does not mean a plea for corporations either in the medieval or the fascist sense. But it is equally impossible to go on conceiving of individuals as millions of abstract atoms without considering the educational and moral significance of their associations.

As long as the various social functions represented by the associations remain uncoordinated and the associations are not considered as an organic part of the community, it is too easy to manipulate the individual by these means. In a hundred ways the modern shrewd technician of influence can reach the individual, as employer or employee, as consumer, student, radio listener, sportsman, or holiday-maker, in days of health or sickness. The result is general disorientation.

The weakening and passing of controls also implies the weakening and passing of liberty. There is no real freedom in the abstract. There are only liberties. Certain types of freedom and restriction belong with each control. The soldier's freedom is different from that of the monk; the teacher's freedom is different from that of the pupil; the father's freedom within his family is different from that in his business relations; and the civil servant's freedom different from that of a free-lance artist or journalist. As long as society functions properly, all are bound by different rules and commitments, but they are also free within the framework of these commitments. What appears as unbridled behavior or license from the point of view of one control may reveal itself as bondage from some other. Where freedom begins for one person, a new type of responsibility exists for another. At first glance, the artist and free-lance journalist seem freer than the soldier or civil servant. But more thorough investigation may reveal that once the soldier and civil servant leave their strictly regulated work they are free of further responsibility and can relax. On the other hand, the artist who seems outwardly free may be bound by the higher responsibilities of his art, and the journalist by his professional code. Qualitative freedom exists only in relation to qualitatively defined commitments. Absolute freedom exists only in anarchy; but this indeed proves that when the laws regulating behavior lose their power of control, freedom, too, is disappearing.

DISINTEGRATION OF COOPERATIVE CONTROLS

The waning power of small communities also results in the vanishing of techniques once so characteristic of them, those of cooperative control.

In any social situation there are two forms of group control. One is the authoritative pattern of command and obedience, the other the pattern of development and guidance of action through cooperation. All the complicated forms of political and social organization on a higher level are derivations of these two original patterns. They are alternative methods for achieving division of labor and differentiation of social functions. The first method, that of command and obedience, very often attains great efficiency but is in most cases detrimental to the individuals concerned. The alternative of cooperation represents a creative principle. This method of shared control is one of the most significant inventions in the field of social techniques. In its conception of a common purpose which can be realized under conditions of shared responsibility, it represents, ancient as it may be, a great advance over the method that forces everyone blindly to follow the commands of one man. Allocation of different tasks in a way that enables everybody to contribute his best should be a comparatively easy division of labor; it is somewhat more difficult to develop cooperative forms of thinking, as in a debate. But in a large-scale society it is extremely difficult to find a cooperative method of creating consensus and sharing common power. Indeed, one of the greatest problems of modern Democracy is to project patterns for establishing consensus and sharing common power in large communities.

In a small sect or community of limited size one can expect all members to sense the spirit of the meeting and find through discussion how much unconscious agreement exists in their minds. However, when the growth of society produces surroundings indicative of class as well as spatial distinctions, with conflicting mental climates, and when the structure of society produces vested interests with organized pressure groups, it becomes increasingly difficult to adhere to the same methods of creating consensus. Those that worked fairly well in the simpler stages of democratic organization scarcely seem adequate now.

The democratic technique of voting tried to replace consensus and the shared responsibility of simpler groups. The institution of voting originated in primitive forms of acclamation, which later became counting of heads and finally led to various schemes of representation, developed with particular skill during the nineteenth century. But those who consider voting and the present system of suffrage the fundamental weapon of democratic control overlook the fact that democratic procedure is vitiated in many ways by manipulated opinion, organized parties, and pressure groups. Moreover, they fail to see that sharing of control is essential not only in the sphere of voting but in all functions and all sections of the community; and we have not yet succeeded in finding methods of sharing controls adequate to the demands of a Great Society.

DISRUPTIVE EFFECTS OF CLASS ANTAGONISM

Left to itself modern society develops a specific kind of disruptive effect from class distinctions and the psychological factors intensifying class antagonisms.

This aspect of modern society has often been discussed and tends to overshadow other causes of disorganization in our social system. It is, indeed, a very significant disruptive force and surely if allowed to develop uncontrolled will lead to class wars and destroy the preconditions of freedom and democratic agreement.

Contrary to the fatalistic belief in the "class struggle," we must emphasize that having developed methods of control that could check growing class differences, we could use them if only we wanted to do so. The obstacles to their application are considerable but essentially no more so than the other disruptive factors discussed. The first step toward mastering this sort of disintegration is to forego the negativist attitude of fatalism and to weigh the pros and cons of a reformist and a revolutionary solution. We shall return to this problem presently.

DISINTEGRATION OF PERSONALITIES

Today we know that we cannot consider separately the disintegration of the primary patterns of cooperation and common life, the deterioration of social controls, the failure to coordinate large-scale organizations, and so on. These are not just institutions gone astray, which some objective procedure of "institutional reconstruction" will set right. Today we know that human conduct and personality formation depend to a large extent on these same institutions. Their disintegration means the disintegration of personality. We expect disorganization of personality where institutions disintegrate because today we know that behavior and character are not abstract entities in themselves but develop primarily out of the context of activities and, to a large extent, out of the institutionalized patterns of cooperative action. That is, if the pattern of cooperation loses its regulative powers, controls are no longer acceptable. They loose their vitality and prestige: accordingly, behavior is bound to disintegrate.

A man who follows traditional patterns unquestioningly is at a complete loss if his belief in tradition is shattered and no new pattern of conduct is at hand to adopt. The same applies when there is a hiatus in the coordination of institutions immediately affecting human behavior.

Most of the commands we obey are supported and sanctioned by groups. There are the army code, professional codes, business codes, and moral codes governing neighborly relations. In modern society, if large organizations fail to develop their own standards, if there are no adequate ethics of industrial relations, no thorough education for citizenship bringing home the virtues of communal responsibility and, finally, if in international relations the law of the jungle prevails, then these lapses will be reflected in the conduct and character of the individuals concerned. People will still behave decently where some remnants of the family code or of the professional code are valid, but will feel lost where the old prescriptions vanish without being replaced by new ones, or where new spheres of life develop that are not yet subject to the moral consciousness of the community. The broader these spheres of lawlessness the more they disintegrate personality, until we reach a stage that Durkheim called *anomie* (*nomos,* law; *a-nomos,* lawlessness). And this is the real state in which people live in a mass society that took the idea of *laissez-faire* literally, not realizing that with the disappearance of older controls, man would be left without orientation. Such a society is morally "undermined."

If we have not yet reached the *anomic* state, it is because the existing undercurrent of tradition and still working and expanding techniques allow agreement on day-to-day issues. But it could be seen how flabby both social conduct and moral character had become, when the first shocks of upheaval came in the shape of war, economic crisis, and inflation. Then the latent perplexity and moral insecurity of the little man came to the fore, and whole nations answered with the desperate cry for "security," the demand for something to hold on to. People considered anybody who promised anything resembling security a prophet, a savior, and a leader whom they would follow blindly rather than remain in a state of utter instability and lawlessness.

DISINTEGRATION OF CONSENSUS AND OF RELIGIOUS BONDS

If our observation is limited to how conduct deteriorates in the context of action, we have not yet fully perceived the disintegration of behavior and personality. By analyzing the causes of social disintegration, we realize that in properly integrated societies there is an additional process at work over and above the formation of conduct and character in action. It is the integrating function of ideological or spiritual inspiration chiefly represented by religion.

When speaking of religion, the sociologist does not mean this or that creed or denomination, but a basic institution which is fairly well expressed in the word 'religion' itself. By derivation *re-ligere* means to "bind closely" whatever you do to a supreme cause. Human activity in the context of living is first woven into a pattern through habits and conventions. But this primary integration is not enough. Man craves a more fundamental oneness relating all his scattered activities to a common purpose. If this commonly accepted purpose disappears, the social machine continues for a while to work as usual since the mutual dependencies and obligations arising from the division of labor do not allow people just to run away. But, whenever a major crisis occurs, it becomes apparent that mutual obligations are only valid if they are rooted in conscience; and conscience, although the most personal experience in man, is a guide to common life only if a moral and religious interpretation of commonly experienced events is accepted and assimilated by the members of that community.

Religion in this sense means linking individual actions and responsibilities to a broader stream of common experience. Religion, therefore, integrates once more on a deeper plane what has already been integrated for limited utilitarian purposes on the more pragmatic level of daily activity.

When religion ceases to be the deeper integrating force in human affairs, the change becomes socially apparent. Until the dissolution of medieval society, religion was alive because it was not only a creed but also a social control inspiring patterns of behavior and ideals of the good life. When this influence was first withdrawn, allowing the state, industry, and other sections of life to take care of themselves, religion lost vigor, and social life found no substitute. First nationalism, then socialism tried to fill this gap. In an age waiting for world integration the self-defeating tendency and harmful influence of nationalism, especially when it becomes an instrument of aggression, are beyond question. Certainly for a time socialism and communism had the power to bind human activities to a higher purpose—that of building a society based upon social justice. But this much is clear: they cannot mean religion for a great part of mankind and thus split instead of uniting men for the next great venture of building a cooperative world society.

The great paradox of any fundamental integration on the plane of *re-ligere* at the present historical juncture is that the so much needed unification of larger communities is too often achieved by antagonism against other religious creeds. These seem to create the kind of zeal and intolerance that with the help of the present perfected tools of warfare can only lead to the extinction of nations.

As long as the world consisted of several units which could develop side by side, religious zeal, time and again, resulted in wars. But those struggles of bygone days seem relatively innocent maneuvers compared with the two world wars, and even more so, in contemplation of the destructive potentialities of wars to come. The criterion of any future spiritual revival as a creative force will be its ability to integrate men without antagonizing them. The fact that this has hardly happened yet cannot be accepted as conclusive by those who believe in the creative powers in man. For in the past man has often shown that he could meet the challenge of an entirely changed environment through the emergence of a completely new mental attitude.

As we contemplate the chaotic state of unregulated capitalist society, one thing becomes quite clear: the present state of society cannot last long. We have seen that social chaos may remain latent so long as no major crisis occurs. But whenever mass unemployment or war brings the tension to a climax, new solutions must be found. By this time the world has learned that such crises are not chance, but that both mass unemployment and wars are inherent in the system. Thus the two basic evils will not disappear without a conscious and systematic attack on them. This of itself indicates that the age of *laissez-faire* is over and that only through planning can catastrophe be avoided.

Internal Difficulties of Democracy

ERNEST BARKER

Ernest Barker, an Oxford political theorist, felt that capitalism and democracy are two coexisting "absolutisms." Confrontation is inevitable; it is absurd to expect that modern Western societies have a choice between the two. Reflections on Government *(1942) was written during the darkest hours of democracy. Yet it expresses the faith of the liberal that capitalism has nothing to fear from democratic political intervention.*

DEMOCRACY in its nature has always carried economic implications. In the days of struggle, when men were agitating for a democratic suffrage and parliamentary institutions, they were also agitating for something which lay behind and beyond their more immediate objects. They did not merely desire the vote; they desired a key to unlock a new world in which the sinister interests of privilege would be corrected, and equal justice, directed to a more equal distribution of happiness, would be established. In the days of achievement, when a general suffrage and a representative parliament had become accomplished facts, the economic consequences of democracy became still clearer. New social classes had been enfranchised; their interests and their desires found public expression; and political reorganization was seen to involve, by a natural and inevitable logic, an increasing measure of social reconstruction. To stop short at political change is to stop in the middle of a river. Few will be content with such a position; and most hands will be outstretched *ripae ulterioris amore* [with longing for the further bank].

The economic consequences of democracy become still more obvious when we consider the new capitalistic epoch of mechanical change and industrial revolution in which it has struggled to birth and in which it is still engaged. In a period of static methods of production and traditional standards of distribution there may

95

be but little incentive to questioning. In a period in which methods of production are rapidly changing and the standards of distribution are constantly changing with them—changing too, as it seems, erratically, and in flat violation of all established tradition —there will be an abundance of questions. It was among such questions that modern democracy was born; we may almost say that it was *from* these questions that it was born. In that sense capitalism—in its modern form, and so far as it has been the parent, or at any rate the brother, of change—has not been hostile to democracy; it has rather been the incentive and stimulus to democratic thought and democratic aspiration. It has produced a vast material which invited and demanded universal discussion; it has led, above everything else, to the institution of systems of government by discussion. Capitalism did not invent democracy in order to govern under its shadow. But it has helped, none the less, to produce it—*malgré lui* [in spite of itself].

But if the questions provided by capitalism have helped to produce democracy, it does not follow that democracy is able to provide the answers to those questions. Apart from the fundamental difficulty, to which we must presently return, that those who have to give the answers are themselves divided by deep divisions of outlook and interest, there is another and minor difficulty, which is none the less becoming increasingly grave and serious. The ultimate result of long years of scientific discovery and mechanical invention, from the steam-engine to wireless telegraphy and the aeroplane, has been an obvious acceleration of the pace of human life. The production and the distribution of wealth have been revolutionized; but that is not the whole of the revolution. Our minds too work with different tools; and a different apparatus of life affects the whole process of deliberation and decision. Rapidity of communication, both physical and mental, has become the mark of our times. Rapidity of communication not only involves a new rapidity of deliberation and decision; it also involves a new and increasing centralization of decision. The great business settles its affairs in the head office; scattered ambassadors, of old almost plenipotentiaries, have become the dependents of the Foreign Office. . . .

There is an old and simple proverb which says, "The more

haste, the less speed." It does not follow from our greater rapidity that we are attaining better solutions, or even that we are attaining any solution. Perhaps all great decisions on cardinal issues are slowly and surely matured. But for our own day, and in this generation, we have to reckon with a mood of impatience, which belongs to a period of rapid mechanical change and may pass away when we settle down into our new environment. This impatience is one of the causes of that "crisis of democracy" which, in turn, is one of the many "crises" among which we live. It leads us to look for sudden salvations and sudden saviours. It throws out of gear, for the time being, the steady process of democratic discussion. With all the means of rapid publicity and instantaneous communication—the talking film, the broadcast voice, the rapid dash by aeroplane—a new system of electric and instantaneous executive leadership now finds its opportunity. Nor is it only the technology of physics, and the new marvels of physical invention, which provide the opportunity. It is also what may be called the technology of psychology. The pure and experimental study of psychology, like the pure and experimental study of physics, is a pure addition to the total sum of human knowledge. But there is a form of technical or applied psychology—the psychology not of the laboratory and the student, but of the market-place and the man of affairs—which has also to be taken into account. It provides a technique which can substitute an induced mass-emotion, by the use of appropriate stimuli, for the rational process of general discussion. When we are taking stock of the influence which applied science, in all its various forms, is exerting upon the conduct and temper of politics, we must not forget the influence of applied psychology. . . .

The material and mechanical changes in the equipment and the pace of life, and their influences on the behaviour of nations and the conduct of national government, form only one aspect of the general revolution of environment which affects all the activity of modern society. There is another and more fundamental aspect, which has already been mentioned, and to which we must now return. The general revolution of environment not only involves physical changes in the equipment and pace of life; it also involves economic changes in the production and distribution of wealth. It is not only a revolution in the world of physics: it is also a revolution in the world of economics. Behind all systems of politics, including the system of democracy, there stands the system of economics. That system, in its present form, presents every system of politics with the profoundest and the most persistent problems which it has to face. But it presents them to democracy in the acutest and most serious form.

There is the problem, in the first place, of the organization of the economic system for its primary purpose of production. That organization, in almost all states, is capitalistic. The owner of capital resources, or the agent who acts on behalf of the owner or a number of associated owners, controls and determines, in virtue of such ownership, the process of production and the action of the workers who are engaged in the process. In its unqualified form, capitalistic organization is a form of autocracy or absolutism. In practice it is never unqualified. On the one hand the legislation of states, whatever the form of their government, generally imposes conditions (beginning with what are called factory laws, but not ending with such laws) on the process of production. On the other hand combinations of workers apply the force of numbers and the menace of a concerted withdrawal of labour to impose further conditions of their own. But the qualified autocracy or absolutism of capitalistic organization still falls short of economic democracy. We may call it, by a contradiction of terms, a limited absolutism, which naturally seeks to escape its limits, and on which (so long as it exists) combinations of workers will as naturally seek to impose new limits.

When we turn from production to the distribution of the product, we are confronted by the same general situation. The owners of capital resources, or the agents for the owners, control and determine, in virtue of such ownership, the process by which the results of industry are distributed in profits and wages. The control is qualified in the same way as the control of the process of production is qualified; though it is seldom qualified (at any rate so far as the action of the state is concerned) to the same extent. On the one hand the state may correct the distribution of the results of production.by instituting a minimum wage for workers, or by limiting profits, or by imposing taxes which largely fall on owners of capital and go to provide social services for the benefit of workers. On the other hand combinations of workers may seek to use their bargaining power to affect the process of distribution in their own favour. By both of these methods, a limited absolutism is again made to take the place of unqualified autocracy.

Democratic states, like other forms of state, have used their authority to limit capitalism by law, and they have left scope to trade unions (though never an absolutely free scope) to impose further limits by the method of collective bargaining with employers. We need not here pause to enquire whether they have imposed *more* limits, or have left trade unions *more* scope to impose further limits, than other forms of states have done. We have to face larger questions. There is, first of all, a question of logic. Can democracy, in its nature, coexist with any form of economic absolutism, however limited? Does it not naturally and logically involve a parallel system of economic democracy, under which the control of production and distribution, in every industry and in every factory, is vested not in a limited autocracy, but in a free partnership of all the agents concerned, who will all determine by common rules, based on a common agreement and attained by a process of common discussion, both the processes of production and the methods of distribution? Such a partnership would not necessarily involve the substitution of a system of social ownership of capital resources for the existing system of private ownership. In other words, it would not necessarily entail the institution of socialism. On the contrary, it would be compatible with the private ownership of capital resources, if only that ownership were diffused, or agreement could be attained that it should be progressively diffused, among all the agents engaged in production. But if the ideal of economic democracy, thus expressed in the form of free partnership, would not necessarily involve the institution of socialism, it would necessarily entail the ending of capitalism in its present form, as a system which vests the control of production and distribution in a body of owners distinct from, and superior to, the other agents concerned in the economic process. We are thus brought to a second question. This is a question of fact and practice. Can any democratic community, as a matter of fact and in actual practice, reasonably hope to achieve, by the democratic process of discussion and compromise, a solution of the economic problem which involves the ending of capitalism in its present form? Is it not too hopelessly divided into two camps, one standing stiffly for the present form of capitalism, and the other standing no less stiffly for the institution of a new system of socialism? We seem to be plunged into a dilemma. On the one hand, democracy ought to secure some economic order of society which is congenial with its own nature and is attained by its own process. On the other hand, its process seems inadequate to attain the solution which is congenial with its nature. The process of debate and compromise seems incapable of attaining that solution, or indeed any solution at all, when there is no common ground on which to debate, and no middle term on which we can compromise.

It is the second of these questions—the question of fact and practice—which is the cardinal question. If the members of a democratic community can agree to think together about a solution of economic problems which agrees with the logic and character of their community, they will find one. We cannot predict the exact solution which they will find, and we cannot lay down in advance the precise conditions to which it must conform. If we seek to do so, we shall be contradicting the spirit of democracy; we shall be saying what men must think, and not leaving them free to think. If we believe in democracy we must believe in the "heuristic" of democracy, and we must not seek to precribe for it exactly what it shall find. The question before us is not therefore the question of the precise nature of the solution which has to be found; it is the question of the capacity for finding *any* solution, when the issue in question is the issue of economics. Can the members of a democratic community agree to think together on that issue, or must they think separately, in two distinct and divided camps? Is it possible, on that issue, and in that respect, to believe in the democratic process and the heuristic of democracy, or are we condemned to disbelief and despair? The answer we give to that question will transcend the immediate economic issue, and will determine our general attitude to the general capacity of democracy. If it cannot solve the greatest of issues, it will stand condemned, whatever the triumphs which it can celebrate, or the hopes which it may nourish, in other fields.

Disraeli, over ninety years ago, published a novel, entitled *Sybil, or the Two Nations.* A few years afterwards, in 1848, Marx and Engels issued the Communist Manifesto, in which the two nations were baptized as the proletariat and the bourgeoisie. Names have power. When once we have taken a notion and given it a sounding name, we readily transplant it from the notional world into the actual, and we vest it with life and motion. The two nations, the proletariat and the bourgeoisie, capital and labour— these names and labels have been turned into living and personal forces, engaged in a struggle which overshadows and dominates everything else. The dualism is simple—too simple to do justice to the multiplicity of actual life, which is not all plain black and white; but its very simplicity is cogent. Under the influence of this dualism it is easy to see everywhere "two and two, one against another." Politics, like the rest of life, can be schematized on this system. There will then be, on the one hand, an organized wealth-owning class, anxious to preserve and increase its wealth, and striving to use the machinery of politics for this object; there will equally be, on the other, an organized non-wealthy class, anxious (under the same impulse of economic necessity) to redistribute wealth, and striving to use the machinery of politics for the achievement of that object. On this basis the process of democracy is subjected to two contrary stresses; and the result of the process will necessarily depend on their relative strength. It will not be common deliberation which will decide economic issues. It will be different and conflicting stresses. When one of the stresses is greater, we shall have what is called capitalistic democracy. When the other is greater, the victory will lie with what is termed social democracy. But there will never be pure and simple democracy. That can never exist after the two antagonists have once entered the scene—or until they both leave it. . . .

THE IDEA OF TWO RIVAL DEMOCRACIES

Are we then to believe in two democracies, and not one; and are we to hold that the two are irretrievably divided? Is that the lesson which we must learn if we place ourselves on the ground of actual reality? In that case we shall have escaped from the over-simplicity of capitalistic democracy only to fall into the utter dualism of two opposed democracies which somehow coexist but cannot cooperate. We shall have one democracy based on the primary principle of private property in capital resources, with all its corollaries; we shall have another based on the primary principle of public ownership of those resources; and since the difference is held to be a difference of primary principle—since it is conceived as turning on the essential first idea which creates and constitutes the whole nature of society—we shall not have a single society in which the two can act, and react, upon one another.

The dualistic picture of life with which we are thus presented is, however, an arbitrary picture, which depends on an arbitrary assumption of the principle of interpretation, and an equally arbitrary selection of the features and facts to be brought into the light and thrown into vivid relief. It is a large assumption of principle when the whole nature of society is made to depend upon its system of ownership. Private property and public ownership are important factors in social life; and a society based on the one will differ in many respects from a society based on the other. But there are also other important factors besides the system of ownership—none of them, indeed, independent of it (any more than it is independent of them), and this for the simple reason that all the factors are interconnected, and necessarily interact, in the common unity of any society. The general scheme of law, which is something larger than the law of property; the faith and the organization of churches; the tradition and the content of general culture—these are all factors in social life; and it is possible to believe that a society which preserves the continuity of these factors may remain fundamentally the same, without undergoing any great change of character, even if it alters radically its system of ownership and its economic basis. We have also to remember, in this connection, that there are few of the older states of the world which are based exclusively on private property. There is no clear distinction between private property states and public ownership states. The economic basis of the political community, in a country such as Great Britain, covers a range which stretches from public ownership and management, through an area of undertakings operating with private capital but subject to public control or even to public management, until it reaches the area of private property and private management. The economic factor, so far as ownership and management is concerned, is accordingly mixed. The two supposed opposites live side by side; systems which are neither live side by side with both; and all amicably play their different parts in the one society. There would be no great change if the balance were gradually tilted towards the side of complete public ownership and public management—provided only that the tilting was due to a process of steady and continuous adjustment, and not to a sudden cataclysm.

When we turn from things and the ownership of things to persons and the status of persons, we are again confronted by the fact of mixture. The dualistic picture of two separate and opposed classes, "two and two, one against another," is an arbitrary picture. The class scheme is an abstraction, drawn from the actual world by the process of selecting some and neglecting other features which it presents, and then imposed upon it as its true form or "idea." It is, in a sense, an artistic or imaginative creation, comparable to the creations of the poet and the painter; but it is not clear that such an imaginative creation can be made the basis of scientific analysis of the present or scientific prediction of the future. If the features and facts which are neglected for the purpose of such creation are both numerous and essential, we may indeed be stirred and moved by the result, as we are moved by a work of art; but such emotion will not be a safe guide to a reasonable and tenable theory of the whole evidence.

The class scheme, with its simple dualism, may be said to omit two sorts of facts which are both essential. Even if we admit the existence of two opposed classes, we have also to admit the existence of other social groups, which are not based on the principle of class, but may none the less cherish their own convictions and formulate their own policies on the issues of economics. Society is not only the home of classes: it is also the home of churches, and of voluntary associations intended for the promotion of social purposes and programmes. The Roman Catholic Church, in every country, gathers its adherents together around its own doctrine of social economics, as that doctrine has been expressed in the encyclicals of 1891 and 1931; and in every country bodies of opinion, formed irrespective of class, and existing for the pure advocacy of some economic plan or some more general social programme, are a part of the general play of social forces. Classes are mixed with other elements—however large they may seem to bulk, they do not occupy the whole field. Political parties, in particular, are forms of voluntary association which exist by the side of class formations, and can only be identified with them by a violent interpretation of their structure and composition. It would hardly be a paradox to maintain that there is nowhere a party which contains all the members of a single class, and contains nothing but the members of that class.

Not only are other social elements mixed with the element of class; that element is itself a mixed and multitudinous thing. Modern life does not present us with any simple cleavage of distinct and separate classes. In the Middle Ages it was possible to distinguish three classes, or forms of status, or "estates"—the baronage, the clergy, and the commons, or, as they were termed in the Latin of the day, the *bellatores,* the *oratores,* and the *laboratores.* In nineteenth century Germany, in which the tradition of the Estates and the *Ständestaat* still survived, it was an easy leap for the theorists of socialism to modify the medieval distinction, and to postulate a plain opposition between the capitalistic class, which had succeeded to the baronage, and a proletarian class which was the depressed heir of the medieval commons. But this modified medievalism did not sit easily on the new industrial age which it professed to describe. The industrial age, with its rapid changes and its new mobility, obliterates the old and simple distinctions of a fixed and static society; but far from putting in their place an even simpler system of distinctions, it substitutes a much more complicated, and a much less stable system. It is true that it consolidates, and thus differentiates, the class of the community which lives by the wages it earns as the price of its manual labour. In that sense the growth of industry may be said to constitute, or at any rate to define and accentuate, a separate proletarian class. But it is far from true that it consolidates, or in any way constitutes, any other single separate class. The more it develops, the more it produces a mixture or complication of social elements. One of these elements may indeed be called capitalistic. But even this element is divided into a financial section, which manipulates capital and credit, and an industrial section which applies a capital that is mainly borrowed to the actual work of production, and the interests of the two sections may disagree with one another. Nor is this all. By the side of this capitalistic element there are also other elements, which may count even more in the general play of society. There are, for example, the professions, which steadily increase not only in numbers, but also in the efficiency of their organization; there are again the technical and managerial staffs in industry (perhaps only a new form or variety of profession), which belong neither to the capitalistic nor to the proletarian side. There is thus no organized single class to confront the class of wage-earning manual workers; there is only a number of different elements; and some of these may feel that their interests, far from separating them from the class of the workers, unite them in harmony with it on many, if not on all, issues. Nor must we exaggerate the homogeneity of the class of manual workers. The interest of one of its sections may conflict with those of others; and many of its members may, by the process of saving and investment, acquire possession of capital and begin to identify their interests with those of other elements of the community. When we consider these facts, we are bound to reject the idea of a necessary dualism of classes. We may even reject the very idea of classes, for the simple reason that we cannot discover any community which is really arranged in a number of distinct and distinguishable classes. "The belief in the existence of social classes," it has been said, "or even of one social class, the interests of the members of which are identical, or nearly so, and opposed to the interests of the rest of the community, is the result of studying social theory of doubtful value and of neglecting social facts."

The study of social facts does not warrant us in believing that there is any unbridgeable gulf (deep as one of the canyons in the New World) between the different social elements contained in the modern state. At the most it might conceivably lead us to conclude, first, that the great body of manual workers has attained a new consolidation (partly through the increasing mechanization of industry, which assimilates the activities of all manual workers in a common process of repetition work, and partly through the parallel development of trade unions, once organized on the basis of different "crafts," into great and comprehensive "industrial" unions which tend to a close alliance); and, secondly, that the other social elements, varied though they may be, are none the less steeped in a common spirit of private property, and dyed in a common colour of private enterprise, which are alien to—or at any rate remote from—the spirit and colour of the world of manual labour. But even if we go to the length of that conclusion—which is, after all, an extreme conclusion, exaggerating the unity of either of the two sides, and exaggerating equally the difference between them—we are not compelled to believe in the doctrine of the unbridgeable gulf, and still less to hold that the state is lodged on one side of the gulf and acts in the interest of that side. The facts testify to the contrary. For at least a century the state, even under a so-called "capitalistic" system (which is really a "mixed" system of private property and public ownership, steadily altering its proportions and its character), has imposed conditions upon the system, which have secured new rights for manual workers, imposed new liabilities on their employers, and restricted the whole of the wealthier section of the community. It has bestridden the gulf, so far as there was a gulf; and, as Solon claimed for himself, it has striven to hold "a strong shield over either side." The record of social legislation cannot be simply dismissed under the facile appellation of "palliatives" or "ransoms" or "sops," as if it were something thrown out, in desperation, to a pack of pursuing wolves. It has been advocated by those who believed, without any *arrière pensée,* in the general and impartial cause of social justice; it has been won, in no small measure, by the honest effort and the concerted strength of the workers themselves, standing for their own rights. Men are driven to curious shifts of interpretation when they seek to make the record of fact fit into the scheme of their own abstractions. The doctrine of ransom or palliatives is one of the most curious of such shifts.

If the state in general does not live on one side of a gulf, but can pass to and fro—bridging, adjusting, and reconciling differences, after its nature and according to its function—there seems to be no fundamental reason for despairing of the democratic form of state. No doubt such a form of state has its own special difficulties. It does not compress social forces and social elements, as the autocratic state is able to do—or rather, can *attempt* to do; it lets them play, and it sets them free to engage in the battle of agitation and debate. It is true that if the forces thus liberated are essentially hostile and fundamentally opposed, their play will be something more than play, and their battle will be more than a battle of agitation and debate. If they are so hostile and so opposed, they will be unable to argue together, because there are no common terms in which they can argue; they will be unable to compromise, because neither is willing to make a concession to the other, or to receive a concession from it. But there is no evidence to prove that the forces which are liberated under the system of democracy necessarily must, or actually do, believe in this stiff and intransigent spirit of buckram logic. It is only intellectual abstractions, "hatched in the schools" of neoscholasticism, which are thus unyielding. In the world of flesh and blood there is always a spirit of accommodation which makes men stretch out tentative hands to find ways and means of living together in some measure of comfort. Good sense has its quiet victories, which, if less renowned, are more substantial than the victories of the remorseless logic of doctrine. The dialectic of practical life is not the dialectic which seeks to refute—it is the dialectic which seeks to persuade.

This temper of accommodation, good sense, and persuasion, is a temper which needs to be cultivated. But we may also say, with no little truth, that it also needs to be left alone. Left to itself, it will produce peace and the fruits of peace. If it be troubled, by constant ingeminations of the doctrine of social war, it may disappear. It is not the social facts of our time which are dangerous, it is rather the social doctrines. It is perfectly possible for democracy to work, and to work well, on the basis of existing social facts and existing social temper. It is possible for a party of the Right and a party of the Left to exist and act in the same society—both acting on democratic principles; each seeking to win a majority; and each willing, if it wins what it seeks, to come to some agreement with the minority, and to make some compromise with it which it will consent to accept. But the possibility may be killed. The spirit of democracy—and with it the system, which can only exist when it is informed by the spirit—may be extinguished. A dualistic abstraction, urged as a gospel, and urged until it creates the reality of dualism, may become the great and compelling factor in human life; and if that happens the presuppositions of democracy will have vanished. There will be no single society: there will be no common terms of debate; there will be differences of opinion far too acute for any agreement to differ, and divisions of policy far too deep to be bridged by any compromise. . . .

The ultimate issue with which we are thus confronted is an issue which transcends the difference between classes, or that between parties, or indeed any difference which is merely a difference of parts or sections of the community. It is an issue between two different spirits, two different tempers of mind—the spirit and temper of accommodation, and the spirit and temper of intransigence. The real war of our times is not a class war: it is a war between two mental worlds. From this point of view we may argue that the fundamental difficulties of democracy are not internal, but external. Democracy belongs to a mental world inspired and controlled by the temper of accommodation—a world that is patient and tolerant of differences, accepting them as the necessary ingredients of unity, and trusting them to achieve it by the method of voluntary adjustment. Belonging to this mental world, democracy is confronted by figures, and forces, and factors, which belong to another. First, there is the figure of the guiding and compelling Hero. Next, there is the force and the exultation of group-sentiment. Lastly, there is the factor of new economic stresses and strains, different from any hitherto studied, which demand, or seem to demand, new and nondemocratic methods of easing. All these belong, in their different ways, to the world of intransigence. The difficulties which they oppose to the successful conduct of democracy are external difficulties; and it is under that head that they must be studied. If democracy is under eclipse in many countries, the fundamental reason is the interposition of another world of ideas, which darkens its sphere and blocks its light.

On Taxation

JONATHAN SWIFT

In Gulliver's Travels *(1726), Jonathan Swift perceived many of man's great follies, including the idea of a "neutral government."*

I HEARD a very warm Debate between two Professors, about the most commodious and effectual Ways and Means of raising Money without grieving the Subject. The first affirmed, the justest Method would be to lay a certain Tax upon Vices and Folly; and the Sum fixed upon every Man, to be rated after the fairest Manner by a Jury of his Neighbours. The second was of an Opinion directly contrary; to tax those Qualities of Body and Mind for which Men chiefly value themselves; the Rate to be more or less according to the Degrees of excelling; the Decision whereof should be left entirely to their own Breast. The highest Tax was upon Men, who are the greatest Favourites of the other Sex; and the Assessments according to the Number and Natures of the Favours they have received; for which they are allowed to be their own Vouchers. Wit, Valour, and Politeness were likewise proposed to be largely taxed, and collected in the same Manner, by every Person giving his own Word for the Quantum of what he possessed. But, as to Honour, Justice, Wisdom and Learning, they should not be taxed at all; because, they are Qualifications of so singular a Kind, that no Man will either allow them in his Neighbour, or value them in himself.

The Women were proposed to be taxed according to their Beauty and Skill in Dressing; wherein they had the same Privilege with the Men, to be determined by their own Judgment. But Constancy, Chastity, good Sense, and good Nature were not rated, because they would not bear the Charge of Collecting. . . .

PART THREE

Public Order: The Role of
Government in America

Report on Manufactures

ALEXANDER HAMILTON

*Alexander Hamilton's greatest state paper, reproduced here in con-
densed form, gives a clear picture of the America of 1791, on the
eve of the Industrial Revolution. The Report expresses that sense
of being on the brink of destiny where for only one moment a real
choice might be made. It also identifies those policies which were
going to characterize American national government for nearly a
century after the Founding.*

THE SECRETARY OF THE TREASURY, in obedience to the order of
the House of Representatives, of the 15th day of January, 1790,
has applied his attention, at as early a period as his other
duties would permit, to the subject of manufactures; and particularly to the means of promoting such as will tend to
render the United States independent of foreign nations for military and other essential supplies. And he thereupon respectfully
submits the following Report.

The expediency of encouraging manufacturers in the United
States, which was not long since deemed very questionable,
appears at this time to be pretty generally admitted. The embarrassments which have obstructed the progress of our external
trade have led to serious reflections on the necessity of enlarging the sphere of our domestic commerce: the restrictive
regulations which in foreign markets abridge the vent of the increasing surplus of our Agricultural produce, serve to beget an
earnest desire that a more extensive demand for that surplus

may be created at home and the complete success which has rewarded manufacturing enterprises in some valuable branches, conspiring with the promising symptoms which attend some less mature essays, in others, justify a hope that the obstacles to the growth of this species of industry are less formidable than they were apprehended to be, and that it is not difficult to find, in its further extension, a full indemnification for any external disadvantages which are or may be experienced, as well as an accession of resources favorable to national independence and safety.

There still are, nevertheless, respectable patrons of opinions, unfriendly to the encouragement of manufactures. The following are, substantially, the arguments by which these opinions are defended.

"In every country (say those who entertain them) agriculture is the most beneficial and *productive* object of human industry. This position, generally, if not universally true, applies with peculiar emphasis to the United States on account of their immense tracts of fertile territory, uninhabited and unimproved. Nothing can afford so advantageous an employment for capital and labor as the conversion of this extensive wilderness into cultivated farms. Nothing equally with this can contribute to the population, strength and real riches of the country.

"To endeavor, by the extraordinary patronage of Government, to accelerate the growth of manufactures is, in fact, to endeavor, by force and art, to transfer the natural current of industry from a more, to a less beneficial channel. Whatever has such a tendency must necessarily be unwise. Indeed it can hardly ever be wise in a government to attempt to give a direction to the industry of its citizens. This under the quicksighted guidance of private interest will, if left to itself, infallibly find its own way to the most profitable employment; and 'tis by such employment that the public prosperity will be most effectually promoted. To leave industry to itself, therefore, is, in almost every case, the soundest as well as the simplest policy.

"This policy is not only recommended to the United States, by considerations which affect all nations; it is, in a manner, dictated to them by the imperious force of a very peculiar situation. The smallness of their population compared with their territory—the constant allurements to emigration from the settled to the unsettled parts of the country—the facility with which the less independent condition of an artisan can be exchanged for the more independent condition of a farmer—these, and similar causes, conspire to produce, and, for a length of time must continue to occasion, a scarcity of hands for manufacturing occupation, and dearness of labor generally. To these disadvantages for the prosecution of manufactures, a deficiency of pecuniary capital being added, the prospect of a successful competition with the manufactures of Europe must be regarded as little less than desperate. Extensive manufactures can only be the offspring of a redundant, at least of a full population. Till the latter shall characterize the situation of this country, 'tis vain to hope for the former.

"If contrary to the natural course of things, an unseasonable and premature spring can be given to certain fabrics, by heavy duties, prohibitions, bounties, or by other forced expedients; this will only be to sacrifice the interests of the community to those of particular classes. Besides the misdirection of labor, a virtual monopoly will be given to the persons employed on such fabrics; and an enhancement of price, the inevitable consequence of every monopoly, must be defrayed at the expense of the other parts of the society. It is far preferable that those persons should be engaged in the cultivation of the earth, and that we should procure, in exchange for its productions, the commodities with which foreigners are able to supply us in greater perfection and upon better terms."

This mode of reasoning is founded upon facts and principles which have certainly respectable pretensions. If it had governed the conduct of nations more generally than it has done, there is room to suppose that it might have carried them faster to prosperity and greatness than they have attained by the pursuit of maxims too widely opposite. Most general theories, however, admit of numerous exceptions, and there are few, if any, of the political kind, which do not blend a considerable portion of error with the truths they inculcate.

In order to an accurate judgment how far that which has been just stated ought to be deemed liable to a similar imputation, it is necessary to advert carefully to the considerations which plead in favor of manufactures, and which appear to recommend the special and positive encouragement of them in certain cases, and under certain reasonable limitations.

It ought readily to be conceded that the cultivation of the earth—as the primary and most certain source of national supply—as the immediate and chief source of subsistence to man —as the principal source of those materials which constitute the nutriment of other kinds of labor—as including a state most favorable to the freedom and independence of the human mind—one, perhaps, most conducive to the multiplication of the human species—has *intrinsically a strong claim to pre-eminence over every other kind of industry.*

But, that it has a title to anything like an exclusive predilection, in any country, ought to be admitted with great caution. That it is even more productive than any other branch of industry requires more evidence than has yet been given in support of the position. That its real interests, precious and important as, without the help of exaggeration, they truly are, will be advanced rather than injured by the due encouragement of manufactures, may, it is believed, be satisfactorily demonstrated. And it is also believed that the expediency of such encouragement in a general view may be shown to be recommended by the most cogent and persuasive motives of national policy. . . .

[At the outset, then, Hamilton faced two opposing views, one represented by Jefferson and one by Adam Smith, which he skillfully paraphrases. Essentially, the first opposing view is that as a way of life agriculture is good and manufacturing is bad. The second view is that, notwithstanding preferences, artificial attempts to divert capital or public attempts to create it are doomed to fail. He evaluates both, paying particular attention to Smith's doubts as to the ultimate success of a *policy* of encouraging manufactures by diverting capital into domestic manufacture and discouraging importation. He does not do full justice to Smith's argument. Hamilton proves adequately that encouraging domestic manufactures would "have the effect of rendering the total mass of useful and productive labor, in a community, greater than it would otherwise be." He never really faces Smith's prediction that the increases of national wealth would be still greater if capital were allowed to flow unchecked into building the agrarian economy that would buy its manufactured goods from Europe. Hamilton's final point can be taken to represent his whole defense.—*Editor*.]

If instead of a farmer and artificer, there were a farmer only, he would be under the necessity of devoting a part of his labor to the fabrication of clothing and other articles, which he would procure of the artificer in the case of there being such a person; and of course he would be able to devote less labor to the cultivation of his farm, and would draw from it a proportionable [*sic*] less product. The whole quantity of production in this state of things, in provisions, raw materials and manufactures, would certainly not exceed in value the amount of what would be produced in provisions and raw materials only, if there were an artificer as well as a farmer.

It is now proper to proceed a step further, and to enumerate the principal circumstances from which it may be inferred that manufacturing establishments not only occasion a positive augmentation of the produce and revenue of the society, but that they contribute essentially to rendering them greater than they could possibly be without such establishments. These circumstances are:

1. The division of labor.
2. An extension of the use of machinery.
3. Additional employment to classes of the community not ordinarily engaged in the business.
4. The promoting of emigration from foreign countries.
5. The furnishing greater scope for the diversity of talents and dispositions which discriminate men from each other.
6. The affording a more ample and various field for enterprise.
7. The creating in some instances a new, and securing in all, more certain and steady demand for the surplus produce of the soil.

Each of these circumstances has a considerable influence upon the total mass of industrious effort in a community. Together, they add to it a degree of energy and effect which are not easily conceived. . . .

To all the arguments which are brought to evince the impracticability of success in manufacturing establishments in the United States, it might have been a sufficient answer to have referred to the experience of what has been already done. It is certain that several important branches have grown up and flourished with a rapidity which surprises, affording an encouraging assurance of success in future attempts. . . .[1]

There remains to be noticed an objection to the encouragement of manufactures, of a nature different from those which question the probability of success. This is derived from its supposed tendency to give a monopoly of advantages to particular classes at the expense of the rest of the community, who, it is affirmed, would be able to procure the requisite supplies of manufactured articles on better terms from foreigners than from our own citizens, and who, it is alleged, are reduced to the necessity of paying an enhanced price for whatever they want, by every measure, which obstructs the free competition of foreign commodities.

It is not an unreasonable supposition that measures which serve to abridge the free competition of foreign articles have a tendency to occasion an enhancement of prices, and it is not to be denied that such is the effect, in a number of cases; but the fact does not uniformly correspond with the theory. A reduction of prices has in several instances immediately succeeded the establishment of a domestic manufacture. Whether it be that foreign manufactures endeavor to supplant, by underselling, our own, or whatever else be the cause, the effect has been such as is stated, and the reverse of what might have been expected.

But though it were true that the immediate and certain effect of regulations controlling the competition of foreign with domes-

1. [Hamilton enumerates "the most considerable" of the successes: tanning and leather goods, various metals and metal products, woodwork, machinery, flax and hemp goods, bricks, liquors, paper, hats, refined sugars, oils and soaps, carriages, snuff, starch and hairpowder, painters' colors, and gunpowder.—*Editor.*]

tic fabrics was increase of price, it is universally true that the contrary is the ultimate effect with every successful manufacture. When a domestic manufacture has attained to perfection, and has engaged in the p. secution of it a competent number of persons, it invariably becomes cheaper. Being free from the heavy charges which attend the importation of foreign commodities, it can be afforded, and accordingly seldom or never fails to be sold cheaper, in process of time, than was the foreign article for which it is a substitute. The internal competition which takes place soon does away [with] every thing like monopoly, and by degrees reduces the price of the article to the *minimum* of a reasonable profit on the capital employed. This accords with the reason of the thing, and with experience.

Whence it follows that it is the interest of a community, with a view to eventual and permanent economy, to encourage the growth of manufactures. In a national view, a temporary enhancement of price must always be well compensated by a permanent reduction of it.

It is a reflection which may with propriety be indulged here, that this eventual diminution of the prices of manufactured articles, which is the result of internal manufacturing establishments, has a direct and very important tendency to benefit agriculture. It enables the farmer to procure, with a smaller quantity of his labor, the manufactured produce of which he stands in need, and consequently increases the value of his income and property. . . .

Not only the wealth, but the independence and security of a country, appear to be materially connected with the prosperity of manufactures. Every nation, with a view to those great objects, ought to endeavor to possess within itself all the essentials of national supply. These comprise the means of *subsistence, habitation, clothing* and *defence*.

The possession of these is necessary to the perfection of the body politic; to the safety as well as to the welfare of the society; the want of either is the want of an important organ of political life and motion; and in the various crises which await a state, it must severely feel the effects of any such deficiency. The extreme embarrassments of the United States during the late war, from an incapacity of supplying themselves, are still matter [*sic*] of keen recollection; a future war might be expected again to exemplify the mischiefs and dangers of a situation to which that incapacity is still in too great a degree applicable, unless changed by timely and vigorous exertion. To effect this change, as fast as shall be prudent, merits all the attention and all the zeal of our public councils; 'tis the next great work to be accomplished. . . .

A full view having now been taken of the inducements to the promotion of manufactures in the United States, accompanied with an examination of the principal objections which are commonly urged in *opposition,* it is proper, in the next place, to consider the means by which it may be effected, as introductory to a specification of the objects which in the present state of things appear the most fit to be encouraged, and of the particular measures which it may be advisable to adopt in respect to each.

In order to a better judgment of the means proper to be resorted to by the United States, it will be of use to advert to those which have been employed with success in other countries. The principal of these are—

I. Protecting Duties—or Duties on Those Foreign Articles Which Are The Rivals of the Domestic Ones Intended to Be Encouraged.

❖   ❖   ❖

II. Prohibitions of Rival Articles, or Duties Equivalent to Prohibitions.

❖   ❖   ❖

III. Prohibitions of the Exportation of the Materials of Manufactures.

❖   ❖   ❖

IV. Pecuniary Bounties.

This has been found one of the most efficacious means of encouraging manufactures, and is, in some views, the best. . . .

A question has been made concerning the constitutional right of the Government of the United States to apply this species of encouragment, but there is certainly no good foundation for such a question. The National Legislature has express authority "To lay and collect taxes, duties, imposts, and excises, to pay the debts, and provide for the *common defence* and *general welfare* with no other qualifications than that "all duties, imposts, and excises shall be *uniform* throughout the United States, and that no capitation or other direct tax shall be laid unless in proportion to numbers ascertained by a census or enumeration taken on the principles prescribed in the Constitution," and that "no tax or duty shall be laid on articles exported from any State."

These three qualifications excepted, the power to *raise money* is *plenary* and *indefinite,* and the objects to which it may be *appropriated* are no less comprehensive than the payment of the public debts, and the providing for the common defence and *general welfare. . . .*

V. Premiums.

Bounties are applicable to the whole quantity of an article produced, or manufactured, or exported, and involve a correspondent expense. Premiums serve to reward some particular excellence or superiority, some extraordinary exertion or skill, and are dispensed only in a small number of cases. But their effect is to stimulate general effort; contrived so as to be both honorary and lucrative, they address themselves to different passions, touching the chords as well of emulation as of interest. They are accordingly a very economical means of exciting the enterprise of a whole community. . . .

VI. The Exemption of the Materials of Manufactures From Duty.

❋   ❋   ❋

VII. Drawbacks of the Duties which Are Imposed on the Materials to Manufactures.[2]

❋   ❋   ❋

VIII. The Encouragement of New Inventions and Discoveries, At Home, And of the Introduction into the United States of

2. [As a rule, Hamilton argued, duties should be kept off raw materials. However, when a raw material, like molasses, is directly consumed as well as serving as a raw material, it might be subject to a tariff. If so, the manufacturers who must use it in production ought to be allowed a "drawback."—*Editor.*]

Such as May Have Been Made in Other Countries; Particularly Those which Relate to Machinery.

This is among the most useful and unexceptionable of the aids which can be given to manufactures. The usual means of that encouragement are pecuniary rewards, and, for a time, exclusive privileges. . . .

IX. Judicious Regulations for the Inspection of Manufactured Commodities.

This is not among the least important of the means by which the prosperity of manufactures may be promoted. It is indeed in many cases one of the most essential. Contributing to prevent frauds upon consumers at home and exporters to foreign countries, to improve the quality and preserve the character of the national manufactures, it cannot fail to aid the expeditious and advantageous sale of them, and to serve as a guard against successful competition from other quarters. . . .

X. The Facilitating of Pecuniary Remittances from Place to Place.

—is a point of considerable moment to trade in general, and to manufactures in particular; by rendering more easy the purchase of raw materials and provisions and the payment for manufactured supplies. A general circulation of bank paper, which is to be expected from the institution lately established [the Bank of the United States] will be a most valuable means to this end. But much good would also accrue from some additional provisions respecting inland bills of exchange. If those drawn in one state payable in another were made negotiable everywhere, and interest and damages allowed in case of protest, it would greatly promote negotiations between the citizens of different states, by rendering them more secure; and with it the convenience and advantage of the merchants and manufacturers of each.[3]

3. [Since Hamilton is not merely "adverting" to those means used in Europe but is really proposing proven means for use in the U. S., it is important to add here his defense of the funded public debt as a relief from "want of capital." See his companion Report on the Public Credit.—*Editor.*]

XI. The Faciliating of the Transportation of Commodities.

＊   ＊   ＊

[This is Hamilton's proposal for what later became a national program of "internal improvements."—*Editor.*]

The great copiousness of the subject of this Report has insensibly led to a more lengthy preliminary discussion than was originally contemplated, or intended. It appeared proper to investigate principles, to consider objections, and to endeavor to establish the utility of the thing proposed to be encouraged, previous to a specification of the objects which might occur, as meriting or requiring encouragement, and of the measures which might be proper in respect to each. The first purpose having been fulfilled, it remains to pursue the second. . . .

A Summary of Hamilton's Program

Objects (a selection)＊	Proposals for Encouragement
Iron & Steel	Duties on rival commodities (except on "iron in pigs and bars")
Nails and Spikes	Nearly prohibitive duties; inspection to prevent "carelessness and dishonesty."
Military Weapons	High duties to protect articles already produced in U. S.; annual stockpiling in arsenals; eventual government manufacture of "all the necessary weapons of war."
Copper, Brass, Lead	Free entry of raw materials, increased duties on all competing wares made of brass, powder & tin.
Coal	Bounties; premiums on the opening of new mines.
Wood (for building)	Eliminate duties; "measures of preservation" of stock, including promotion of magazines of ship timber.
Grain and Spirits	Greatly increase duties, especially on imported spirits; reduce taxes on domestic spirits,† duties on malt liquors sufficient to prohibit importation of all but the highest quality; prohibitory duties on "articles of starch, hair powder and wafers."

＊ [Other objects singled out for encouragement but not included in this summary are: silk, glass, paper, sugar, chocolate, and manufactured products

A Summary of Hamilton's Program—Cont.

Objects (a selection)*	Proposals for Encouragement
Flax and Hemp	Protective duties; bounties or premiums on such manufactured articles as sail cloth.
Cotton	Repeal duties on import or raw cotton to encourage manufacture; bounties on domestic cotton and on goods produced from it; bounty on exported cotton; duties on import finished goods with drawbacks for domestic printers and dyers.
Wool	Premiums on domestic, "with an eye to quality as well as quantity"; bounties on imports; finance these by adding 2½ per cent duty on carpeting.
Gun Powder	Free import on ingredients; "regulations for the careful inspection of" sulphur.

related to them; printed books; and many other manufactured products related to those materials included in this summary.—*Editor.*]

† [This includes the infamous "whiskey tax."—*Editor.*]

The measures. . .which have been submitted, taken aggregatively, will for a long time to come rather augment than decrease the public revenue. . .[A]ll the additional duties which shall be laid [will not only adequately substitute for those to be reduced or abolished]. . .but will yield a considerable surplus. . . .

In countries where there is great private wealth, much may be effected by the voluntary contributions of patriotic individuals; but in a community situated like that of the United States, the public purse must supply the deficiency of private resource. In what can it be so useful, as in prompting and improving the efforts of industry?

All which is humbly submitted.

The Lochner Dissent *

OLIVER WENDELL HOLMES, ASSOCIATE JUSTICE

Hamilton's government was patron, subsidizer, benefactor of private husbandry. In Holmes's dissent there is another government —one responsive to a mass, and one prepared to enter into coercive and directive relationships with public order. Does our Constitution place any barrier against such rule?

[Lochner, a baker, was convicted of violating a New York labor law, which provided that no employee could be "required or permitted" to work in a baking establishment more than sixty hours per week or more than ten hours in any one day. The majority of the Supreme Court in *Lochner* v. *New York* invalidated the statute on the grounds that it was an interference with the rights of "grown and intelligent men," both employees and employers, to enter into contracts for employment. There was insufficient damage to health or the cleanliness of bread to warrant use of state police powers, in the absence of which, the freedom of master and servant to enter into contracts could not be interferred with, without violating the federal Constitution as the majority interpreted it.]

MR. JUSTICE HOLMES IN DISSENTING SAID:

I regret sincerely that I am unable to agree with the judgment in this case, and I think it my duty to express my dissent.

This case is decided upon an economic theory which a large part of the country does not entertain. If it were a question whether I agreed with that theory, I should desire to study it further and long before making up my mind. But I do not conceive that to be my duty, because I strongly believe that my agreement or disagreement has nothing to do with the right of a majority to embody their opinions in law. It is settled by vari-

* [198 U. S. 45; 49 L. Ed. 937; 25 Sup. Ct. 539. 1905]

ous decisions of this Court that state constitutions and state laws may regulate life in many ways which we as legislators might think as injudicious or if you like as tyrannical as this, and which equally with this interfere with the liberty to contract. Sunday laws and usury laws are ancient examples. A more modern one is the prohibition of lotteries. The liberty of the citizen to do as he likes so long as he does not interfere with the liberty of others to do the same, which has been a shibboleth for some well-known writers, is interfered with by school laws, by the postoffice, by every state or municipal institution which takes his money for purposes thought desirable, whether he likes it or not.

The Fourteenth Amendment does not enact Mr. Herbert Spencer's Social Statics.[1] The other day we sustained the Massachusetts vaccination law.[2] United States and state statutes and decisions cutting down the liberty to contract by way of combination are familiar to this court.[3] Two years ago we upheld the prohibition of sales of stock on margins or for future delivery in the constitution of California.[4] The decision sustaining an eight-hour law for miners is still recent.[5] Some of these laws embody convictions or prejudices which judges are likely to share. Some may not. But a constitution is not intended to embody a particular economic theory, whether of paternalism and the organic relation of the citizen to the state or of laissez faire. It is made for people of fundamentally differing views, and the accident of our finding certain opinions natural and familiar or novel and even shocking ought not to conclude our judgment upon the question whether statutes embodying them conflict with the Constitution of the United States.

General propositions do not decide concrete cases. The decision will depend on a judgment or intuition more subtle than any articulate major premise. But I think that the proposition just stated, if it is accepted, will carry us far toward the end.

1. [See Introduction—*Editor.*]
2. *Jacobson v. Massachusetts,* 197 U. S. 11.
3. *Northern Securities Co. v. United States,* 193 U. S. 197.
4. *Otis v. Parker,* 187 U. S. 606.
5. *Holden v. Hardy,* 169 U. S. 366.

Every opinion tends to become a law. I think that the word "liberty" in the Fourteenth Amendment is perverted when it is held to prevent the natural outcome of a dominant opinion, unless it can be said that a rational and fair man necessarily would admit that the statute proposed would infringe fundamental principles as they have been understood by the traditions of our people and our law. It does not need research to show that no such sweeping condemnation can be passed upon the statute before us. A reasonable man might think it a proper measure on the score of health. Men whom I certainly could not pronounce unreasonable would uphold it as a first instalment of a general regulation of the hours of work. Whether in the latter aspect it would be open to the charge of inequality I think it unnecessary to discuss.

To Secure These Rights

THE PRESIDENT'S COMMITTEE ON CIVIL RIGHTS

Modern government seems to be run on the assumption that for every right there must be a remedy, even when no direct Constitutional authority can be found. In one of our most important twentieth-century state papers, President Truman's Committee (1947) exemplifies contemporary analysis of constitutional law.

THE CONSTITUTION, as it came from the Philadelphia Convention in 1787, granted to Congress no express power to enact civil rights legislation of any kind. Moreover, the first ten Amendments, which make up our Bill of Rights, far from granting any positive powers to the federal government, serve as express limitations upon it. The Thirteenth, Fourteenth, and Fifteenth Amendments added to the Constitution immediately following the close of the Civil War do expressly authorize Congress to pass laws in certain civil rights areas. But the areas are of limited extent and are not clearly defined. Thus, there is nothing in the Constitution which in so many words authorizes the national government to protect the civil rights of the American people on a comprehensive basis. . . .

There are [however] several specific constitutional bases upon which a federal civil rights program can be built. Some have been recognized and approved by the courts. Others have the support of leading students of the American constitutional system. Some are beyond dispute; others are frankly controversial. Collectively, however, they provide an encouraging basis for action. The President and Congress must determine the wisdom of a broader civil rights program at the policy level. They should be advised that such a program, carefully framed, will meet the test of constitutionality.

The several specific constitutional bases for federal action in the civil rights field brought to our attention follow. Those numbered from one through eight have either been specifically approved by the Supreme Court or seem to be clearly valid. Those numbered from nine through eleven are more controversial and will be discussed at greater length.

1. *Power to protect the right to vote.* The extent of federal power to protect the suffrage varies, depending on the type of election (state or national), the type of interference (whether it affects the voting procedure, or is based on race or sex) and the source of interference (state and local officers or private persons). Among the specific sources of federal power are: Article I, Section 4, which permits federal protection of the procedure for voting in federal elections against interference from any source; the Fourteenth Amendment which supports protection against state interference with equality of opportunity to vote in any election; the Fifteenth Amendment which supports action against state interference because of race or color with the right to vote in any election; and the Nineteenth Amendment, which supports action against state interference based on sex with the right to vote in any election.

2. *Power to protect the right to freedom from slavery and voluntary servitude.* This power derives from the Thirteenth Amendment: "Neither slavery nor involuntary servitude, except as a punishment for crime whereof the party shall have been duly convicted, shall exist within the United States, or any place subject to their jurisdiction." This permits legislation designed to protect against action of private persons or state or local officials.

3. *Power to protect rights to fair legal process, to free speech and assembly, and to equal protection of the laws.* This power derived from the "due process," "equal protection" and "privileges or immunities" clauses of the Fourteenth Amendment, cannot be readily summarized, except for the fact that, under Supreme Court rulings, it protects only against interferences by agencies of state or local government. In a wide variety of specific situations —such as cases involving the validity of ordinances licensing the distribution of handbills, the adequacy of representation by counsel, or the validity of state laws or administrative action claimed to discriminate against minorities—the Supreme Court has delineated areas of activity protected by these constitutional provisions.

Congress is expressly authorized to enact legislation to implement this power, and has passed some statutes for this purpose.

4. *The war power.* Under Section 8 of Article I of the Constitution Congress has extensive power to regulate the armed forces and to legislate concerning the national defense and security. Congress may thus legislate with respect to treatment of minority groups in the services, with respect to interference with members of the services, and with respect to construction or operation of military and naval installations. Related is the congressional power to assure distribution of veterans' benefits on an equal basis.

5. *Power to regulate activities which relate to interstate commerce.* Congress has exercised its broad power to regulate interstate commerce, derived from Article I, Section 8 of the Constitution, to institute reforms in many fields. Outstanding examples are the Fair Labor Standards Act, which fixes maximum hours and minimum wages in work relating to interstate commerce, the National Labor Relations Act, which regulates labor-management relations affecting interstate commerce, and the Federal Safety Appliance Act, which specifies safety standards for interstate transportation. The commerce power could be the basis for fair employment legislation relating to activities affecting interstate commerce, and for laws prohibiting discriminatory practices by interstate carriers.

6. *The taxing and spending powers.* Also derived from Article I, Section 8, these are among the most extensive congressional powers, and have been repeatedly used to effectuate federal programs. An outstanding example is the Social Security program. Federal grants-in-aid have almost always been conditioned on compliance with congressionally declared standards, as have exemptions from taxation. Congress has power to impose similarly appropriate conditions in spending or taxing programs which affect civil rights problems. Another facet of these powers permits Congress to require persons who enter into contracts with the federal government, or supply the government with goods or services to conform with national policy. For example, in the Walsh-Healey Act, Congress has made compliance with minimum wage and maximum hour standards a condition of perform-

ance of federal supply contracts.

7. *The postal power.* Under its plenary power over the postal system (stemming from Article I, Section 8) Congress has acted to protect use of the mails against certain undesirable purposes. This power is, of course, subject to the constitutional limits on congressional power to impair free speech. Within those limits, however, there may be room for certain types of legislation—such as the exclusion of anonymous hate group literature from the mails.

8. *Power over the District of Columbia and the Territories.* Under Article I, Section 8 and Article IV, Section 3, Congress has full power of government over the District of Columbia and the various territories. It may thus pass any legislation proper for complete protection of the civil rights of all persons residing in those areas.

9. *Power derived from the Constitution as a whole to protect the rights essential to national citizens in a democratic nation.* No such power is expressly granted to Congress in the Constitution. It has long been asserted that the basic rights falling into this category, such as freedom of speech and press or the right of assembly, exist at the state level and depend upon state action for their protection against interference by private persons. However, the Supreme Court long ago suggested that such rights have a national significance as exercised in connection with the national political process, and that they may be protected by national legislation. . . .

As recently as 1940, the Fifth Circuit Court of Appeals in the case of *Powe* v. *United States,* in a dictum said:

Because the federal government is a republican one in which the will of the people ought to prevail, and because that will ought to be expressive of an informed public opinion, the freedom of speaking and printing on subjects relating to that government, its elections, its laws, its operations and its officers is vital to it.

And the court said that Congress has power under the Constitution to protect freedom of discussion, so defined, against all threats.

Unfortunately, these dicta have not been directly tested in

practice. It is impossible to say how far the courts may be willing to go in recognizing the existence of specific rights at the national level, or in approving the power of Congress to protect these rights as necessary to a democratic nation. But the basis seems to be a valid one and it might support national civil rights legislation of considerable significance.

10. *Power derived from the treaty clause in Article II, Section 2 of the Constitution, to protect civil rights which acquire a treaty status.* In its decision in *Missouri v. Holland* in 1920, the Supreme Court ruled that Congress may enact statutes to carry out treaty obligations, even where, in the absence of a treaty, it has no other power to pass such a statute. This doctrine has an obvious importance as a possible basis for civil rights legislation.

The United Nations Charter, approved by the United States Senate as a treaty, makes several references to human rights. Articles 55 and 56 are of particular importance. . . .

A strong argument can be made under the precedent of *Missouri v. Holland* that Congress can take "separate action" to achieve the purposes set forth in Article 55 by passing legislation designed to secure "respect for, and observance of, human rights and fundamental freedoms for all without distinction as to race, sex, language, or religion." . . .

11. *Power derived from the "republican form of government" clause in Article IV, Section 4 of the Constitution, to protect rights essential to state and local citizens in a democracy.* This clause reads "The United States shall guarantee to every State in this Union a republican form of government. . . ." This phraseology is admittedly vague, and has had relatively little interpretation by the Supreme Court. But other vague clauses of the Constitution, such as the commerce clause or the due process of law clauses, have lent themselves to broad interpretation. It is possible that guaranteeing "a republican form of government" includes the power to protect essential civil rights against interference by public officers or private persons.

In view of this analysis of the Constitution, both as to its broad character and its more specific clauses, the Committee believes that federal legislation in support of civil liberty is legitimate and well within the scope of the Constitution. . . .

The Flag Salute Case *

ROBERT H. JACKSON

In the 1930s the Supreme Court finally acceded to the principle that the democratic process ought not to be limited. However, this aristocratic Branch has held valiantly to one check against popular rule, expressed in this excerpt by the brilliant Justice Jackson (1943). Nonetheless, it can be seen from this case how reluctant the Court is to hamstring the legislature.

MR. JUSTICE JACKSON delivered the opinion of the Court:

Following the decision by this Court in *Minersville School District* v. *Gobitis,* 310 U. S. 586, the West Virginia legislature amended its statutes to require all schools therein to conduct courses of instruction in history, civics, and in the Constitutions of the United States and of the state "for the purpose of teaching, fostering and perpetuating the ideals, principles and spirit of Americanism, and increasing the knowledge of the organization and machinery of the government." Appellant Board of Education was directed, with advice of the State Superintendent of Schools, to "prescribe the courses of study covering these subjects" for public schools. The Act made it the duty of private, parochial and denominational schools to prescribe courses of study "similar to those required for the public schools."

The Board of Education on January 9, 1942, adopted a resolution containing recitals taken largely from the Court's Gobitis opinion and ordering that the salute to the flag become "a regular part of the program of activities in the public schools," that all teachers and pupils "shall be required to participate in the salute honoring the Nation represented by the Flag; provided, however, that refusal to salute the Flag be regarded as an Act of insubordination, and shall be dealt with accordingly." . . .

* [*West Virginia State Board of Education* v. *Barnette* (319 U. S. 624; 87 L. Ed. 1628; 63 Sup. Ct. 1178. 1943.)]

Appellees, citizens of the United States and of West Virginia, brought suit in the United States District Court for themselves and others similarly situated asking its injunction to restrain enforcement of these laws and regulations against Jehovah's Witnesses. The Witnesses are an unincorporated body teaching that the obligation imposed by law of God is superior to that of laws enacted by temporal government. Their religious beliefs include a literal version of Exodus, Chapter 20, verses 4 and 5, which says: "Thou shalt not make unto thee any graven image, or any likeness of anything that is in heaven above, or that is in the earth beneath, or that is in the water under the earth; thou shalt not bow down thyself to them, nor serve them." They consider that the Flag is an "image" within this command. For this reason they refuse to salute it.

Children of this faith have been expelled from school and are threatened with exclusion for no other cause. Officials threaten to send them to reformatories maintained for criminally inclined juveniles. Parents of such children have been prosecuted and are threatened with prosecutions for causing delinquency. . . .

The freedom asserted by these appellees does not bring them into collision with rights asserted by any other individual. It is such conflicts which most frequently require intervention of the state to determine where the rights of one end and those of another begin. But the refusal of these persons to participate in the ceremony does not interfere with or deny rights of others to do so. Nor is there any question in this case that their behavior is peaceable and orderly. The sole conflict is between authority and rights of the individual. The state asserts power to condition access to public education on making a prescribed sign and profession and at the same time to coerce attendance by punishing both parent and child. The latter stand on a right of self-determination in matters that touch individual opinion and personal attitude. . . .

As the present Chief Justice [Stone] said in dissent in the Gobitis case, the state may "require teaching by instruction and study of all in our history and in the structure and organization of our government, including the guaranties of civil liberty, which tend to inspire patriotism and love of country." Here, however, we are dealing with a compulsion of students to declare a belief. They are not merely made acquainted with the flag salute so that they may be informed as to what it is or even what it means. The issue here is whether this slow and easily neglected route to arouse loyalties constitutionally may be short-cut by substituting a compulsory salute and slogan. . . .

There is no doubt that, in connection with the pledges, the flag salute is a form of utterance. Symbolism is a primitive but effective way of communicating ideas. The use of an emblem or flag to symbolize some system, idea, institution, or personality, is a short cut from mind to mind. Causes and nations, political parties, lodges and ecclesiastical groups seek to knit the loyalty of their followings to a flag or banner, a color or design. The state announces rank, function, and authority through crowns and maces, uniforms and black robes; the church speaks through the Cross, the Crucifix, the altar and shrine, and clerical raiment. Symbols of state often convey political ideas just as religious symbols come to convey theological ones. Associated with many of these symbols are appropriate gestures of acceptance or respect: a salute, a bowed or bared head, a bended knee. A person gets from a symbol the meaning he puts into it, and what is one man's comfort and inspiration is another's jest and scorn.

Over a decade ago Chief Justice Hughes led this Court in holding that the display of a red flag as a symbol of opposition by peaceful and legal means to organize government was protected by the free speech guaranties of the Constitution.[1] Here it is the state that employs a flag as a symbol of adherence to government as presently organized. It requires the individual to communicate by word and sign his acceptance of the political ideas it thus bespeaks. Objection to this form of communication when coerced is an old one, well known to the framers of the Bill of Rights.

It is also to be noted that the compulsory flag salute and pledge requires affirmation of a belief and an attitude of mind. It is not clear whether the regulation contemplates that pupils forego any contrary convictions of their own and become unwilling converts to the prescribed ceremony or whether it will be acceptable if they simulate assent by words without belief and

1. *Stromberg* v. *California*, 283 U. S. 359.

a gesture barren of meaning. It is now a commonplace that censorship or suppression of expression of opinion is tolerated by our Constitution only when the expression presents a clear and present danger of action of a kind the state is empowered to prevent and punish. It would seem that involuntary affirmation could be commanded only on even more immediate and urgent grounds than silence. But here the power of compulsion is invoked without any allegation that remaining passive during the flag salute ritual creates a clear and present danger that would justify an effort even to muffle expression. To sustain the compulsory flag salute we are required to say that a Bill of Rights which guards the individual's right to speak his own mind, left it open to public authorities to compel him to utter what is not in his mind.

Whether the First Amendment to the Constitution will permit officials to order observance of ritual of this nature does not depend upon whether as a voluntary exercise we would think it to be good, bad or merely innocuous. Any credo of nationalism is likely to include what some disapprove or to omit what others think essential, and to give off different overtones as it takes on different accents or interpretations. If official power exists to coerce acceptance of any patriotic creed, what it shall contain cannot be decided by courts, but must be largely discretionary with the ordaining authority, whose power to prescribe would no doubt include power to amend. Hence validity of the asserted power to force an American citizen publicly to profess any statement of belief or to engage in any ceremony of assent to one, presents questions of power that must be considered independently of any idea we may have as to the utility of the ceremony in question.

Nor does the issue as we see it turn on one's possession of particular religious views or the sincerity with which they are held. While religion supplies appellees' motive for enduring the discomforts of making the issue in this case, many citizens who do not share these religious views hold such a compulsory rite to infringe constitutional liberty of the individual. It is not necessary to inquire whether nonconformist beliefs will exempt from the duty to salute unless we first find power to make the salute a legal duty.

The Gobitis decision, however, *assumed,* as did the argument in that case and in this, that power exists in the state to impose the flag salute discipline upon school children in general. The Court only examined and rejected a claim based on religious beliefs of immunity from an unquestioned general rule. The question which underlies the flag salute controversy is whether such a ceremony so touching matters of opinion and political attitude may be imposed upon the individual by official authority under powers committed to any political organization under our Constitution. We examine rather than assume. existence of this power and, against this broader definition of issues in this case, reexamine specific grounds assigned for the Gobitis decision.

It was said that the flag salute controversy confronted the Court with "the problem which Lincoln cast in memorable dilemma: 'Must a government of necessity be too *strong* for the liberties of its people, or too *weak* to maintain its own existence?'" and that the answer must be in favor of strength.[2]

We think these issues may be examined free of pressure or restraint growing out of such considerations.

It may be doubted whether Mr. Lincoln would have thought that the strength of government to maintain itself would be impressively vindicated by our confirming power of the state to expel a handful of children from school. Such oversimplification, so handy in political debate, often lacks the precision necessary to postulates of judicial reasoning. If validly applied to this problem, the utterance cited would resolve every issue of power in favor of those in authority and would require us to override every liberty thought to weaken or delay execution of their policies.

Government of limited power need not be anemic government. Assurance that rights are secure tends to diminish fear and jealousy of strong government, and by making us feel safe to live under it makes for its better support. Without promise of a limiting Bill of Rights it is doubtful if our Constitution could have mustered enough strength to enable its ratification. To enforce those rights today is not to choose weak government over strong government. It is only to adhere as a means of strength to individual freedom of mind in preference to officially disciplined

2. *Minersville School District* v. *Gobitis, op. cit.*

uniformity for which history indicates a disappointing and disastrous end.

The subject now before us exemplifies this principle. Free public education, if faithful to the ideal of secular instruction and political neutrality, will not be partisan or enemy of any class, creed, party, or faction. If it is to impose any ideological discipline, however, each party or denomination must seek to control, or failing that, to weaken the influence of the educational system. Observance of the limitations of the Constitution will not weaken government in the field appropriate for its exercise.

It was also considered in the Gobitis case that functions of educational officers in states, counties and school districts were such that to interfere with their authority "would in effect make us the school board for the country."

The Fourteenth Amendment, as now applied to the state, protects the citizen against the state itself and all of its creatures—boards of education not excepted. These have, of course, important, delicate, and highly discretionary functions, but none that they may not perform within the limits of the Bill of Rights. That they are educating the young for citizenship is reason for scrupulous protection of constitutional freedoms of the individual, if we are not to strangle the free mind at its source and teach youth to discount important principles of our government as mere platitudes.

Such boards are numerous and their territorial jurisdiction often small. But small and local authority may feel less sense of responsibility to the Constitution, and agencies of publicity may be less vigilant in calling it to account. The action of Congress in making flag observance voluntary and respecting the conscience of the objector in a matter so vital as raising the Army contrasts sharply with these local regulations in matters relatively trivial to the welfare of the nation. There are village tyrants as well as village Hampdens, but none who acts under color of law is beyond reach of the Constitution.

The Gobitis opinion reasoned that this is a field "where courts possess no marked and certainly no controlling competence," that it is committed to the legislatures as well as the courts to guard cherished liberties and that it is constitutionally appropriate to "fight out the wise use of legislative authority in the forum of public opinion and before legislative assemblies rather than to transfer such a contest to the judicial arena," since all the "effective means of inducing political changes are left free."

The very purpose of a Bill of Rights was to withdraw certain subjects from the vicissitudes of political controversy, to place them beyond the reach of majorities and officials and to establish them as legal principles to be applied by the courts. One's right to life, liberty, and property, to free speech, a free press, freedom of worship and assembly, and other fundamental rights may not be submitted to vote; they depend on the outcome of no elections.

In weighing arguments of the parties it is important to distinguish between the due process clause of the Fourteenth Amendment as an instrument for transmitting the principles of the First Amendment and those cases in which it is applied for its own sake. The test of legislation which collides with the Fourteenth Amendment, because it also collides with the principles of the First, is much more definite than the test when only the Fourteenth is involved. Much of the vagueness of the due process clause disappears when the specific prohibitions of the First become its standard. The right of a state to regulate, for example, a public utility may well include, so far as the due process test is concerned, power to impose all of the restrictions which a legislature may have a "rational basis" for adopting. But freedoms of speech and of press, of assembly, and of worship may not be infringed on such slender grounds. They are susceptible of restriction only to prevent grave and immediate danger to interests which the state may lawfully protect. It is important to note that while it is the Fourteenth Amendment which bears directly upon the state it is the more specific limiting principles of the First Amendment that finally govern this case.

Nor does our duty to apply the Bill of Rights to assertions of official authority depend upon our possession of marked competence in the field where the invasion of rights occurs. True, the task of translating the majestic generalities of the Bill of Rights, conceived as part of the pattern of liberal government in the eighteenth century, into concrete restraints on officials dealing with the problems of the twentieth century, is one to disturb self-confidence. These principles grew in soil which also produced a philosophy that the individual was the center of society, that his liberty was attainable through mere absence of governmental restraints, and that government should be entrusted with few controls and only the mildest supervision over men's affairs. We must transplant these rights to a soil in which the laissez-faire concept or principle of noninterference has withered at least as to economic affairs, and social advancements are increasingly sought through closer integration of society and through expanded and strengthened governmental controls. These changed conditions often deprive precedents of reliability and cast us more than we would choose upon our own judgment. But we act in these matters not by authority of our competence but by force of our commissions. We cannot, because of modest estimates of our competence in such specialties as public education, withhold the judgment that history authenticates as the function of this Court when liberty is infringed.

Lastly, and this is the very heart of the Gobitis opinion, it reasons that "national unity is the basis of national security," that the authorities have "the right to select appropriate means for its attainment," and hence reaches the conclusion that such compulsory measures toward "national unity" are constitutional. Upon the verity of this assumption depends our answer in this case.

National unity as an end which officials may foster by persuasion and example is not in question. The problem is whether under our Constitution compulsion as here employed is a permissible means for its achievement.

Struggles to coerce uniformity of sentiment in support of some end thought essential to their time and country have been waged by many good as well as by evil men. Nationalism is a relatively recent phenomenon but at other times and places the ends have been racial or territorial security, support of a dynasty or regime, and particular plans for saving souls. As first and moderate methods to attain unity have failed, those bent on its accomplishment must resort to an ever increasing severity. As governmental pressure toward unity becomes greater, so strife becomes more bitter as to whose unity it shall be. Probably no deeper division of our people could proceed from any provocation than from finding it necessary to choose what doctrine and whose program public educational officials shall compel youth to unite in embracing. Ultimate futility of such attempts to compel coherence is the lesson of every such effort from the Roman drive to stamp out Christianity as a disturber of its pagan unity, the Inquisition, as a means to religious and dynastic unity, the Siberian exiles as a means to Russian unity, down to the fast failing efforts of our present totalitarian enemies. Those who begin coercive elimination of dissent soon find themselves exterminating dissenters. Compulsory unification of opinion achieves only the unanimity of the graveyard.

It seems trite but necessary to say that the First Amendment to our Constitution was designed to avoid these ends by avoiding these beginnings. There is no mysticism in the American concept of the state or of the nature or origin of its authority. We set up government by consent of the governed, and the Bill of Rights denies those in power any legal opportunity to coerce that consent. Authority here is to be controlled by public opinion, not public opinion by authority.

The case is made difficult not because the principles of its decision are obscure but because the flag involved is our own. Nevertheless, we apply the limitations of the Constitution with no fear that freedom to be intellectually and spiritually diverse or even contrary will disintegrate the social organization. To believe that patriotism will not flourish if patriotic ceremonies are voluntary and spontaneous instead of a compulsory routine is to make an unflattering estimate of the appeal of our institutions to free minds. We can have intellectual individualism and the rich cultural diversities that we owe to exceptional minds only at the price of occasional eccentricity and abnormal attitudes. When they are so harmless to others or to the state as those we deal with here, the price is not too great. But freedom to differ is not limited to things that do not matter much. That would be a mere shadow of freedom. The test of its substance is the right to differ as to things that touch the heart of the existing order.

If there is any fixed star in our constitutional constellation, it is that no official, high or petty, can prescribe what shall be orthodox in politics, nationalism, religion, or other matters of opinion or force citizens to confess by word or act their faith therein. If there are any circumstances which permit an exception, they do not now occur to us.

We think the action of the local authorities in compelling the flag salute and pledge transcends constitutional limitations on their power and invades the sphere of intellect and spirit which it is the purpose of the First Amendment . . . to reserve from all official control.

The decision of this Court in Minersville School District v. Gobitis . . . [is] overruled, and the judgment enjoining enforcement of the West Virginia Regulation is affirmed.

MR. JUSTICE BLACK and MR. JUSTICE DOUGLAS, concurring:

We are substantially in agreement with the opinion just read, but since we originally joined with the Court in the Gobitis case, it is appropriate that we make a brief statement of reasons for our change of view.

Reluctance to make the Federal Constitution a rigid bar against state regulation of conduct thought inimical to the public welfare was the controlling influence which moved us to consent to the Gobitis decision. Long reflection convinced us that although the principal is sound, its application in the particular case was wrong.[3] We believe that the statute before us fails to accord full scope to the freedom of religion secured to the appellees by the First and Fourteenth Amendments. . . .

No well-ordered society can leave to the individuals an absolute right to make final decisions, unassailable by the State, as to everything they will or will not do. The First Amendment does not go so far. Religious faiths, honestly held, do not free individuals from responsibility to conduct themselves obediently to laws which are either imperatively necessary to protect society as a whole from grave and pressingly imminent dangers or which, without any general prohibition, merely regulate time, place or manner of religious activity. Decision as to the constitutionality of particular laws which strike at the substance of religious tenets and practices must be made by this Court. The duty is a solemn one, and in meeting it we cannot say that a failure, because of

3. *Jones* v. *Opelika,* 316 U. S. 584, 623.

religious scruples, to assume a particular physical position and to repeat the words of a patriotic formula creates a grave danger to the nation. Such a statutory exaction is a form of test oath, and the test oath has always been abhorrent in the United States. . . .

MR. JUSTICE FRANKFURTER, dissenting:

One who belongs to the most vilified and persecuted minority in history is not likely to be insensible to the freedoms guaranteed by our Constitution. Were my purely personal attitude relevant I should wholeheartedly associate myself with the general libertarian views in the Court's opinion, representing as they do the thought and action of a lifetime. But as judges we are neither Jew nor Gentile, neither Catholic nor agnostic. We owe equal attachment to the Constitution and are equally bound by our judicial obligations whether we derive our citizenship from the earliest or the latest immigrants to these shores. As a member of this Court I am not justified in writing my private notions of the policy into the Constitution, no matter how deeply I may cherish them or how mischievous I may deem their disregard. The duty of a judge who must decide which of two claims before the Court shall prevail, that of a State to enact and enforce laws within its general competence or that of an individual to refuse obedience because of the demands of his conscience, is not that of the ordinary person. It can never be emphasized too much that one's own opinion about the wisdom or evil of a law should be excluded altogether when one is doing one's duty on the bench. The only opinion of our own even looking in that direction that is material is our opinion whether legislators could in reason have enacted such a law. In the light of all the circumstances, including the history of this question in this Court, it would require more daring than I possess to deny that reasonable legislators could have taken the action which is before us for review. Most unwillingly, therefore, I must differ from my brethren with regard to legislation like this. I cannot bring my mind to believe that the "liberty" secured by the Due Process Clause gives this Court authority to deny to the State of West Virginia the attainment of that which we all recognize as a legitimate legislative end, namely, the promotion of good citizenship, by employment of the means here chosen. . . .

Came the Revolution

In a New York Times *book review of the paper-bound edition of
Keynes's* General Theory, *John Kenneth Galbraith—Harvard professor, Ambassador to India, key intellectual in the Democratic
party—traces out the rise of the new orthodoxy. Here we begin
to see the background of new policies that are fundamentally
altering the relation of American government to public order.*

THE MOST influential book on economic and social policy so far in
this century, *The General Theory of Employment, Interest, and
Money,* by John Maynard Keynes, was published 29 years ago
last February in Britain and a few weeks later in the United
States. A paperback edition is now available here for the first time,
and quite a few people who take advantage of this bargain will
be puzzled at the reason for the book's influence. Though com-
fortably aware of their own intelligence, they will be unable to
read it. They will wonder, accordingly, how it persuaded so many
other people—not all of whom, certainly, were more penetrating
or diligent. This was only one of the remarkable things about this
book and the revolution it precipitated.

By common, if not yet quite universal agreement, the Keynesian revolution was one of the great modern accomplishments in
social design. It brought Marxism in the advanced countries to a
total halt. It led to the level of economic performance that now
inspires bitter-end conservatives to panegyrics of unexampled
banality. Yet those responsible have had no honors and some opprobrium. For a long while, to be known as an active Keynesian
was to invite the wrath of those who equate social advance with
subversion. Those concerned developed a habit of reticence. As a
further consequence, the history of the revolution is, perhaps, the
worst-told story of our era.

It is time that we knew better this part of our history and

those who made it, and this is a little of the story. Much of it turns on the almost unique unreadability of *The General Theory* and hence the need for people to translate and propagate its ideas to government officials, students and the public at large. As Messiahs go, Keynes was deeply dependent on his prophets. . . .

It is a measure of how far the Keynesian revolution has proceeded that the central thesis of *The General Theory* now sounds rather commonplace. Until it appeared, economists, in the classical (or non-socialist) tradition, had assumed that the economy, if left to itself, would find its equilibrium at full employment. Increases or decreases in wages and the interest rates would occur as necessary to bring about this pleasant result. If men were unemployed, their wages would fall in relation to prices. With lower wages and wider margins, it would be profitable to employ those from whose toil an adequate return could not previously have been made. It followed that steps to keep wages at artificially high levels, such as might result from the ill-considered efforts by unions, would cause unemployment. Such efforts were deemed to be the principal cause of unemployment.

Movements in interest rates played a complementary role by insuring that all income would ultimately be spent. Thus, were people to decide for some reason to increase their savings, the interest rates on the now more abundant supply of loanable funds would fall. This, in turn, would lead to increased investment. The added outlays for investment goods would offset the diminished outlays by the more frugal consumers. In this fashion, changes in consumer spending or in investment decisions were kept from causing any change in total spending that would lead to unemployment.

Keynes argued that neither wage movements nor changes in the rate of interest had, necessarily, any such agreeable effect. He focused attention on the total of purchasing power in the economy—what freshmen are now taught to call aggregate demand. Wage reductions might not increase employment; in conjunction with other changes, they might merely reduce this aggregate demand. And he held that interest was not the price that was paid to people to save but the price they got for exchanging holdings of cash, or its equivalent, their normal preference in assets, for less liquid forms of investment. And it was difficult to reduce interest beyond a certain level. Accordingly, if people sought to save more, this would not necessarily mean lower interest rates and a resulting increase in investment. Instead, the total demand for goods might fall, along with employment and also investment, until savings were brought back into line with investment by the pressure of hardship which had reduced saving in favor of consumption. The economy would find its equilibrium not at full employment but with an unspecified amount of unemployment.

Out of this diagnosis came the remedy. It was to bring aggregate demand back up to the level where all willing workers were employed, and this could be accomplished by supplementing private expenditure with public expenditure. This should be the policy wherever intentions to save exceeded intentions to invest. Since public spending would not perform this offsetting role if there were compensating taxation (which is a form of saving), the public spending should be financed by borrowing—by incurring a deficit. So far as Keynes can be condensed into a few paragraphs, this is it. *The General Theory* is more difficult. There are nearly 400 pages, some of them of fascinating obscurity.

Before the publication of *The General Theory*, Keynes had urged his ideas directly on President Roosevelt, most notably in a famous letter to The New York Times on December 31, 1933: "I lay overwhelming emphasis on the increase of national purchasing power resulting from government expenditure which is financed by loans." And he visited F.D.R. in the summer of 1934 to press his case, although the session was no great success; each, during the meeting, seems to have developed some doubts about the general good sense of the other.

In the meantime, two key Washington officials, Marriner Eccles, the exceptionally able Utah banker who was to become head of the Federal Reserve Board, and Lauchlin Currie, a former Harvard instructor who was director of research and later an economic aide to Roosevelt (and later still a prominent victim of McCarthyite persecution), had on their own account reached conclusions similar to those of Keynes as to the proper course of fiscal policy. When *The General Theory* arrived, they took it as confirmation of the course they had previously been urging. Currie, a highly qualified economist and teacher, was also a skilled and influential interpreter of the ideas in the Washington community. Not often have important new ideas on economics entered a government by way of its central bank. Nor should conservatives worry. There is not the slightest indication that it will ever happen again.

Paralleling the work of Keynes in the thirties and rivaling it in importance, though not in fame, was that of Simon Kuznets and a group of young economists and statisticians at the University of Pennsylvania, the National Bureau of Economic Research and the U.S. Department of Commerce. They developed the now familiar concepts of National Income and Gross National Product and their components and made estimates of their amount. Included among the components of National Income and Gross National Product was the saving, investment, aggregate of disposable income and the other magnitudes of which Keynes was talking. As a result, those who were translating his ideas into action knew not only what needed to be done, but how much. And many who would never have been persuaded by the Keynesian abstractions were compelled to belief by the concrete figures from Kuznets and his inventive colleagues.

However, the trumpet—if the metaphor is permissible for this particular book—that was sounded in Cambridge, England was heard most clearly in Cambridge, Massachusetts. Harvard was the principal avenue by which Keynes's ideas passed to the United States. Conservatives worry about universities being centers of disquieting innovation. Their worries are surely exaggerated—but it has occurred.

In the late thirties, Harvard had a large community of young economists, most of them held there by the shortage of jobs that Keynes sought to cure. They had the normal confidence of their years in their ability to remake the world and, unlike less fortunate generations, the opportunity. They also had occupational indication of the need. Massive unemployment persisted year after year. It was degrading to have to continue telling the young that this was merely a temporary departure from the full employment norm, and that one need only obtain the needed wage reductions.

Paul Samuelson of the Massachusetts Institute of Technology, who, almost from the outset, was the acknowledged leader of the younger Keynesian community, has compared the excitement of the young economists, on the arrival of Keynes's book, to that of Keats on first looking into Chapman's Homer. Some will wonder if economists are capable of such refined emotion, but the effect was certainly great. Here was a remedy for the despair that could be seen just beyond the Yard. It did not overthrow the system but saved it. To the nonrevolutionary, it seemed too good to be true. To the occasional revolutionary, it was. The old economics was still taught by day. But in the evening, and almost every evening from 1936 on, almost everyone discussed Keynes.

This might, conceivably, have remained a rather academic discussion. As with the Bible and Marx, obscurity stimulated abstract debate. But in 1938, the practical instincts that economists sometimes suppress with success were catalyzed by the arrival at Harvard from Minnesota of Alvin H. Hansen. He was then about 50, an effective teacher and a popular colleague. But most of all he was a man for whom economic ideas had no standing apart from their use.

The economists of established reputation had not taken to Keynes. Faced with the choice between changing one's mind and proving that there is no need to do so, almost everyone opts for the latter. So it was then. Hansen had an established reputation, and he did change his mind. Though he had been an effective critic of some central propositions in Keynes's *Treatise on Money,* an immediately preceding work, and was initially rather cool to *The General Theory,* he soon became strongly persuaded of its importance.

He proceeded to expound the ideas in books, articles and lectures and to apply them to the American scene. He persuaded his students and younger colleagues that they should not only understand the ideas but win understanding in others and then go on to get action. Without ever seeking to do so or being quite aware of the fact, he became the leader of a crusade. In the late thirties Hansen's seminar in the new Graduate School of Public Administration was regularly visited by the Washington policy makers. Often the students overflowed into the hall. One felt that it was the most important thing currently happening in the country and this could have been the case.

The officials took Hansen's ideas, and perhaps even more his sense of conviction, back to Washington. In time there was also a strong migration of his younger colleagues and students to the capital. Among numerous others were Richard Gilbert, now a principal architect of Pakistan's economic development, who was a confidant of Harry Hopkins; Richard Musgrave, now of Princeton, who applied Keynes's and Hansen's ideas to the tax system; Alan Sweezy, now of California Institute of Technology, who went to the Federal Reserve and the W.P.A.; George Jaszi, who went to the Department of Commerce; Griffiths Johnson, who served at the Treasury, National Resources Planning Board and the White House; and Walter Salant, now of the Brookings Institution, who served in several Federal agencies. Keynes himself once wrote admiringly of this group of young Washington disciples.

The discussions that had begun in Cambridge continued through the war years in Washington. . . .

Meanwhile, others were concerning themselves with a wider audience. Seymour Harris, another of Hansen's colleagues and an early convert to Keynes, became the most prolific exponent of the ideas in the course of becoming one of the most prolific scholars of modern times. He published half a dozen books on Keynes and outlined the ideas in hundreds of letters, speeches, memoranda, Congressional appearances and articles. Professor Samuelson, mentioned above, put the Keynesian ideas into what became (and remains) the most influential textbook on economics since the last great exposition of the classical system by Alfred Marshall. . . .

In 1946, ten years after the publication of *The General Theory,* the Employment Act of that year gave the Keynesian system the qualified but still quite explicit support of law. It recognized, as Keynes had urged, that unemployment and insufficient output would respond to positive policies. Not much was said about the specific policies but the responsibility of the Federal Government to act in some fashion was clearly affirmed. The Council of Economic Advisers became, in turn, a platform for expounding the Keynesian view of the economy and it was brought promptly into use. Leon Keyserling, as an original member and later chairman, was a tireless exponent of the ideas. And he saw at an early stage the importance of enlarging them to embrace not only the prevention of depression but the maintenance of an adequate rate of economic expansion. Thus in a decade had the revolution spread.

Those who nurture thoughts of conspiracy and clandestine plots will be saddened to know that this was a revolution without organization. All who participated felt a deep sense of personal responsibility for the ideas; there was a varying but deep urge to persuade. But no one ever responded to plans, orders, instructions, or any force apart from his own convictions. That perhaps was the most interesting single feature of the Keynesian revolution.

Something more was, however, suspected. And there was some effort at counterrevolution. Nobody could say that he preferred massive unemployment to Keynes. And even men of conservative mood, when they understood what was involved, opted for the policy—some asking only that it be called by some other name. The Committee for Economic Development, coached by Beardsley Ruml on semantics, never advocated deficits. Rather it spoke well of a budget that was balanced only under conditions of high employment. Those who objected to Keynes were also invariably handicapped by the fact that they had not (and could not) read the book. It was like attacking the original *Kama Sutra* for obscenity without being able to read Sanskrit. Still, where social change is involved, there are men who can surmount any handicap.

Appropriately Harvard, not Washington, was the principal object of attention. In the fifties, a group of graduates of mature years banded together in an organization called the Veritas Foundation and produced a volume called *Keynes at Harvard*. It found that "Harvard was the launching pad for the Keynesian rocket in America." But then it damaged this not implausible proposition by identifying Keynesianism with socialism, Fabian socialism, Marxism, Communism, Fascism and also literary incest, meaning that one Keynesian always reviewed the works of another Keynesian. . . .

As a somewhat less trivial matter, another and more influential group of graduates pressed for an investigation of the Department of Economics, employing as their instrument the visiting committee that annually reviews the work of the department on behalf of the Governing Boards. The Keynesian revolution belongs to our history; so accordingly does this investigation.

It was conducted by Clarence Randall, then the exceptionally articulate head of the Inland Steel Company, with the support of Sinclair Weeks, a manufacturer, former Senator and tetrarch of the right wing of the Republican Party in Massachusetts. In due course, the committee found that Keynes was, indeed, exerting a baneful influence on the Harvard economic mind and that the department was unbalanced in his favor. As always, there was the handicap that the investigators, with one or two possible exceptions, had not read the book and were otherwise uncertain as to what they attacked. The department, including the members most skeptical of Keynes's analysis—no one accepted all of it and some very little—unanimously rejected the committee's finding. So, as one of his last official acts before becoming High Commissioner to Germany, did President James Bryant Conant. There was much bad blood.

In ensuing years there was further discussion of the role of Keynes at Harvard and of related issues. But it became increasingly amicable, for the original investigators had been caught up in one of those fascinating and paradoxical developments with which the history of the Keynesian (and doubtless all other) revolutions is replete. Shortly after the committee reached its disturbing conclusion, the Eisenhower Administration came to power.

Mr. Randall became a Presidential assistant and adviser. Mr. Weeks became Secretary of Commerce and almost immediately was preoccupied with the firing of the head of the Bureau of Standards over the question of the efficacy of Glauber's salts as a battery additive. Having staked his public reputation against the nation's scientists and engineers on the issue (as the late Bernard De Voto put it) that a battery could be improved by giving it a laxative, Mr. Weeks could hardly be expected to keep open another front against the economists. But much worse, both he and Mr. Randall were acquiring a heavy contingent liability for the policies of the Eisenhower Administration. And these, it soon developed, had almost as strong a Keynesian coloration as the department at Harvard.

President Eisenhower's first Chairman of the Council of Economic Advisers was Arthur F. Burns of Columbia University and the National Bureau of Economic Research. Mr. Burns had credentials as a critic of Keynes. In his introduction to the 1946 annual report of the National Bureau, called "Economic Research and the Keynesian Thinking of Our Times," he had criticized a version of the Keynesian underemployment equilibrium and concluded a little heavily that "the imposing schemes for governmental action that are being bottomed on Keynes's equilibrium theory must be viewed with skepticism." Alvin Hansen had replied rather sharply.

But Burns was (and is) an able economist. If he regarded Keynes with skepticism, he viewed recessions (including ones for which he might be held responsible) with positive antipathy. In his 1955 Economic Report, he said, "Budget policies can help promote the objective of maximum production by wisely allocating resources *first between private and public uses;* second, among various government programs." (Italics added by Galbraith.) Keynes, reading these words carefully, would have strongly applauded. And, indeed, a spokesman for the National Association of Manufacturers told the Joint Economic Committee that they pointed "directly toward the planned and eventually the socialized economy."

After the departure of Burns, the Eisenhower Administration incurred a deficit of no less than $9.4 billions in the national income accounts in the course of overcoming the recession of 1958. This was by far the largest deficit ever incurred by an American Government in peacetime; it exceeded the *total* peacetime expenditure by F.D.R. in any year up to 1940. No Administration before or since has given the economy such a massive dose of Keynesian medicine. With a Republican Administration, guided by men like Mr. Randall and Mr. Weeks, following such policies, the academic Keynesians were no longer vulnerable. Keynes ceased to be a wholly tactful topic of conversation with such critics.

Presidents Kennedy and Johnson have continued what is now commonplace policy. Advised by Walter Heller, a remarkably skillful exponent of Keynes's ideas, they added the new device of the deliberate tax reduction to sustain aggregate demand. And they abandoned, at long last, the doubletalk by which advocates of Keynesian policies combined advocacy of measures to promote full employment and economic growth with promises of a promptly balanced budget. "We have recognized as self-defeating the effort to balance our budget too quickly in an economy operating well below its potential," President Johnson said in his 1965 report.

Now, as noted, Keynesian policies are the new orthodoxy. Economists are everywhere to be seen enjoying their new and pleasantly uncontroversial role. Like their predecessors who averted their eyes from unemployment, many are now able to ignore—often with some slight note of scholarly righteousness—the new problem, which is an atrocious allocation of resources between private wants and public needs, especially those of our cities. (In a sense, the Keynesian success has brought back an older problem of economics, that of resource allocation, in a new form.) And there is the dangerously high dependence on military spending. But these are other matters.

We have yet to pay proper respect to those who pioneered the Keynesian revolution. Everyone now takes pride in the resulting performance of the economy. We should take a little pride in the men who brought it about. It is hardly fitting that they should have been celebrated only by the reactionaries. The debt to the courage and intelligence of Alvin Hansen is especially great. Next only to Keynes, his is the credit for saving what even conservatives still call capitalism.

Measures for a Stronger Economy

JOHN F. KENNEDY

President Kennedy's 1962 Economic Report took something of an ultimate step in the fusion of Keynesian doctrines and modern bureaucracies. Here he asks for three important means by which the Executive, in his own discretion, may direct the economy. Could conservatives have any grounds for their fears that the expansion of democratic government cannot be stopped, once begun?

To the Congress of the United States:

I report to you under the provisions of the Employment Act of 1946 at a time when

—the economy has regained its momentum;

—the economy is responding to the Federal Government's efforts, under the Act, "to promote maximum employment, production, and purchasing power";

—the economy is again moving toward the central objective of the Act—to afford "useful employment opportunities, including self-employment, for those able, willing, and seeking to work."

My first Economic Report is an appropriate occasion to reemphasize my dedication to the principles of the Employment Act. As a declaration of national purpose and as a recognition of Federal responsibility, the Act has few parallels in the nation's history. In passing the Act by heavy bipartisan majorities, the Congress registered the consensus of the American people that this nation will not countenance the suffering, frustration, and injustice of unemployment, or let the vast potential of the world's leading economy run to waste in idle manpower, silent machinery, and empty plants.

The framers of the Employment Act were wise to choose the promotion of "maximum employment, production, and purchasing power" as the keystone of national economic policy. They were confident that these objectives can be effectively promoted "in a manner calculated to foster and promote free competitive enterprise and the general welfare." They knew that our pursuit of maximum employment and production would be tempered with compassion, with justice, and with a concern for the future. But they knew also that the other standards we set for our economy are easier to meet when it is operating at capacity. A full employment economy provides opportunities for useful and satisfying work. It rewards enterprise with profit. It generates saving for the future and transforms it into productive investment. It opens doors for the unskilled and underprivileged and closes them against want and frustration. The conquest of unemployment is not the sole end of economic policy, but it is surely an indispensable beginning.

The record of the economy since 1946 is a vast improvement over the prolonged mass unemployment of the 1930's. The Employment Act itself deserves no small part of the credit. Under the mandate and procedures of the Act, both Congress and the Executive have kept the health of the national economy and the economic policies of the Government under constant review. And the national commitment to high employment has enabled business firms and consumers to act and to plan without fear of another great depression.

Though the postwar record is free of major depression, it is marred by four recessions. In the past fifteen years, the economy has spent a total of seven years regaining previous peaks of industrial production. In two months out of three, 4 per cent or more of those able, willing, and seeking to work have been unable to find jobs. We must do better in the 1960's.

To combat future recessions—to keep them short and shallow if they occur—I urge adoption of a three-part program for sustained prosperity, which will (1) provide stand-by power, subject to congressional veto, for temporary income tax reductions, (2) set up a stand-by program of public capital improvements, and (3) strengthen the unemployment insurance system.

These three measures will enable the Government to counter swings in business activity more promptly and more powerfully than ever before. They will give new and concrete meaning to the declaration of policy made in the Employment Act. They will constitute the greatest step forward in public policy for economic stability since the Act itself. . . .

GOALS OF ECONOMIC POLICY

Though we may take satisfaction with our progress to date, we dare not rest content. The unfinished business of economic policy includes (1) the achievement of full employment and sustained prosperity without inflation, (2) the acceleration of economic growth, (3) the extension of equality of opportunity, and (4) the restoration of balance of payments equilibrium. Economic policy thus confronts a demanding assignment, but one which can and will be met within the framework of a free economy.

Our Goal of Full and Sustained Prosperity without Inflation • Recovery has carried the economy only part of the way to the goal of "maximum production, employment, and purchasing power." The standing challenge of the Employment Act is not merely to do better, but to do our best—the "maximum." Attainment of that maximum in 1963 would mean a GNP of approximately $600 billion, wages and salaries of over $320 billion, and corporate profits of as much as $60 billion, all in 1961 prices. The material gains are themselves staggering, but they are less important than the new sense of purpose and the new opportunities for improvement of American life that could be realized by "maximum" use of the productive capacity now lying idle and the capacity yet to be created.

Involuntary unemployment is the most dramatic sign and disheartening consequence of underutilization of productive capacity. It translates into human terms what may otherwise seem merely an abstract statistic. We cannot afford to settle for any prescribed level of unemployment. But for working purposes we view a 4 per cent unemployment rate as a temporary target. It can be achieved in 1963, if appropriate fiscal, monetary, and other policies are used. The achievable rate can be lowered still further by effective policies to help the labor force acquire the skills and mobility appropriate to a changing economy. We must also continue the cooperative effort, begun with the Area Redevelopment Act of 1961, to bring industry to depressed areas and jobs to displaced workers. Ultimately, we must reduce unemployment to the minimum compatible with the functioning of a free economy.

We must seek full recovery without endangering the price stability of the last four years. The experience of the past year has shown that expansion without inflation is possible. With cooperation from labor and management, I am confident that we can go on to write a record of full employment without inflation.

The task of economic stabilization does not end with the achievement of full recovery. There remains the problem of keeping the economy from straying too far above or below the path of steady high employment. One way lies inflation, and the other way lies recession. Flexible and vigilant fiscal and monetary policies will allow us to hold the narrow middle course.

Our Goal of Economic Growth • While we move toward full and sustained use of today's productive capacity, we must expand our potential for tomorrow. Our postwar economic growth—though a step ahead of our record for the last half-century—has been slowing down. We have not in recent years maintained the 4 to 4½ per cent growth rate which characterized the early postwar period. We should not settle for less than the achievement of a long-term growth rate matching the early postwar record. Increasing our growth rate to 4½ per cent a year lies within the range of our capabilities during the 1960's. It will lay the groundwork for meeting both our domestic needs and our world responsibilities.

In November of last year we joined with our nineteen fellow members of the Organization for Economic Cooperation and Development in setting a common target for economic growth. Together we pledged ourselves to adopt national and international policies aimed at increasing the combined output of the Atlantic Community by 50 per cent between 1960 and 1970. The nations of the West are encouraged and enlivened by America's determination to make its full contribution to this joint effort.

We can do our share. In the mid-1960's, the children born in 1943 and after will be arriving at working age. The resulting rapid growth in our labor force offers us an opportunity, not a burden—provided that we deliver not only the jobs but also the research, the training, and the capital investment to endow our new workers with high and rising productivity as they enter economic life.

Our Goal of Equal Opportunity • Increasingly in our lifetime, American prosperity has been widely shared and it must continue so. The spread of primary, secondary, and higher education, the wider availability of medical services, and the improved postwar performance of our economy have bettered the economic status of the poorest families and individuals.

But prosperity has not wiped out poverty. In 1960, 7 million families and individuals had personal incomes lower than $2,000. In part, our failure to overcome poverty is a consequence of our failure to operate the economy at potential. The incidence of unemployment is always uneven, and increases in unemployment tend to inflict the greatest income loss on those least able to afford it. But there is a claim on our conscience from others, whose poverty is barely touched by cyclical improvements in general economic activity. To an increasing extent, the poorest families in America are those headed by women, the elderly, nonwhites, migratory workers, and the physically or mentally handicapped—people who are shortchanged even in time of prosperity.

Last year's increase in the minimum wage is evidence of our concern for the welfare of our low-income fellow citizens. Other legislative proposals now pending will be particularly effective in improving the lot of the least fortunate. These include (1) health insurance for the aged, financed through the social security system, (2) Federal aid for training and retraining our employed and underemployed workers, (3) the permanent strengthening of our unemployment compensation system, and (4) substantial revision in our public welfare and assistance program, stressing rehabilitation services which help to restore families to independence.

Public education has been the great bulwark of equality of opportunity in our democracy for more than a century. Our schools have been a major means of preventing early handicaps from hardening into permanent ignorance and poverty. There can be no better investment in equity and democracy—and no better instrument for economic growth. For this reason, I urge action by the Congress to provide Federal aid for more adequate public school facilities, higher teachers' salaries, and better quality in education. I urge early completion of congressional action on the bill to authorize loans for construction of college academic facilities and to provide scholarships for able students who need help. The talent of our youth is a resource which must not be wasted.

Finally, I shall soon propose to the Congress an intensive program to reduce adult illiteracy, a handicap which too many of our fellow citizens suffer because of inadequate educational opportunities in the past.

Our Goal of Basic Balance in International Payments • Persistent international payments deficits and gold outflows have made the balance of payments a critical problem of economic policy. We must attain a balance in our international transactions which permits us to meet heavy obligations abroad for the security and development of the free world, without continued depletion of our gold reserves or excessive accumulation of short-term dollar liabilities to foreigners. Simultaneously, we must continue to reduce barriers to international trade and to increase the flow of resources from developed to developing countries. To increase our exports is a task of higher priority, and one which gives heightened significance to the maintenance of price stability and the rapid increase of productivity at home. . . .

A PROGRAM FOR SUSTAINED PROSPERITY

Recurrent recessions have thrown the postwar American economy off stride at a time when the economics of other major industrial countries have moved steadily ahead. To improve our future performance I urge the Congress to join with me in erecting a defense-in-depth against future recessions. The basic elements of this defense are (1) Presidential stand-by authority for prompt, temporary income tax reductions, (2) Presidential stand-by authority for capital improvements expenditures, and (3) a permanent strengthening of the unemployment compensation system.

In our free enterprise economy, fluctuations in business and consumer spending will, of course, always occur. But this need not doom us to an alteration of lean years and fat. The business cycle does not have the inevitability of the calendar. The Government can time its fiscal transactions to offset and to dampen fluctuations in the private economy. Our fiscal system and budget policy already contribute to economic stability, to a much greater degree than before the war. But the time is ripe, and the need apparent, to equip the Government to act more promptly, more flexibly, and more forcefully to stabilize the economy—to carry out more effectively its charge under the Employment Act.

Stand-by Tax Reduction Authority • First, I recommend the enactment of stand-by authority under which the President, subject to veto by the Congress, could make prompt temporary reductions in the rates of the individual income tax to combat recessions, as follows:

1. Before proposing a temporary tax reduction, the President must make a finding that such action is required to meet the objectives of the Employment Act.
2. Upon such finding, the President would submit to Congress a proposed temporary uniform reduction in all individual income tax rates. The proposed temporary rates may not be more than 5 percentage points lower than the rates permanently established by the Congress.
3. This change would take effect thirty days after submission, unless rejected by a joint resolution of the Congress.
4. It would remain in effect for six months, subject to revision or renewal by the same process or extension by a joint resolution of the Congress.

5. If the Congress were not in session, a Presidentially proposed tax adjustment would automatically take effect but would terminate thirty days after the Congress reconvened. Extension would require a new proposal by the President, which would be subject to congressional veto.

A temporary reduction of individual income tax rates across the board can be a powerful safeguard against recession. It would reduce the annual rate of tax collections by $2 billion per percentage point, or a maximum of $10 billion—$1 billion per point, or a $5-billion maximum, for six months—at present levels of income. These figures should be measured against the costs they are designed to forestall:

—the tens of billions of potential output that run to waste in recession;
—the pain and frustration of the millions whom recessions throw out of work;
—the Budget deficits of $12.4 billion in fiscal 1959 or $7.0 billion this year.

The proposed partial tax suspension would launch a prompt counterattack on the cumulative forces of recession. It would be reflected immediately in lower withholding deductions and higher take-home pay for millions of Americans. Markets for consumer goods and services would promptly feel the stimulative influence of the tax suspension.

It would offer strong support to the economy for a timely interval, while preserving the revenue-raising powers of our tax system in prosperity and the wise traditional procedures of the Congress for making permanent revisions and reforms in the system. I am not asking the Congress to delegate its power to levy taxes, but to authorize a temporary and emergency suspension of taxes by the President—subject to the checkrein of Congressional veto—in situations where time is of the essence.

Stand-by Capital Improvement Authority • Second, I recommend that the Congress provide stand-by authority to the President to accelerate and initiate up to $2 billion of appropriately timed capital improvements when unemployment is rising, as follows:

1. The President would be authorized to initiate the program within two months after the seasonally adjusted unemployment rate

   a had risen in at least three out of four months (or in four out of six months) and

   b had risen to a level at least one percentage point higher than its level four months (or six months) earlier.

2. Before invoking this authority, the President must make a finding that current and prospective economic developments require such action to achieve the objectives of the Employment Act.

3. Upon such finding, the President would be authorized to commit

   a up to $750 million in the acceleration of direct Federal expenditures previously authorized by the Congress,

   b up to $750 million for grants-in-aid to State and local governments,

   c up to $250 million in loans to States and localities which would otherwise be unable to meet their share of project costs, and

   d up to $250 million additional to be distributed among the above three categories as he might deem appropriate.

4. The authority to initiate new projects under the capital improvements program would terminate automatically within twelve months unless extended by the Congress—but the program could be terminated at any time by the President.

5. Grants-in-aid would be made under rules prescribed by the President to assure that assisted projects (*a*) were of high priority, (*b*) represented a net addition to existing State and local expenditures, and (*c*) could be started and completed quickly.

6. Expenditures on Federal projects previously authorized by the Congress would include resource conservation and various Federal public works, including construction, repair, and modernization of public buildings.

7. After the program had terminated, the authority would not again be available to the President for six months.

The above criteria would have permitted Presidential authority to be invoked in the early stages of each of the four postwar recessions—within four months after the decline had begun. Furthermore, no false signals would have been given. Were a false signal to occur—for example, because of a strike—the authority, which is discretionary, need not be invoked.

The first impact of the accelerated orders, contracts, and outlays under the program would be felt within one to two months after the authority was invoked. The major force of the program would be spent well before private demand again pressed hard on the economy's capacity to produce. With the indicated safeguards, this program would make a major contribution to business activity, consumer purchasing power, and employment in a recession by utilizing for sound public investment resources that would otherwise have gone to waste.

Unemployment Compensation • Third, I again urge the Congress to strengthen permanently our Federal-State system of unemployment insurance. My specific recommendations include

1. Extension of the benefit period by as much as thirteen weeks for workers with at least three years of experience in covered employment;
2. Similar extension of the benefit period when unemployment is widespread for workers with less than three years of experience in covered employment. This provision could be put into effect by Presidential proclamation when insured unemployment reaches 5 per cent, and the number of benefit exhaustions over a three-month period reaches 1 per cent of covered employment;
3. Incentives for the States to provide increased benefits, so that the great majority of covered workers will be eligible for weekly benefits equal to at least half of their average weekly wage;
4. Extension of coverage to more than three million additional workers;
5. Improved financing of the program by an increase in the wage base for the payroll tax from $3,000 to $4,800;

6. Reinsurance grants to States experiencing high unemployment insurance costs;

7. Provisions which permit claimants to attend approved training or retraining courses without adverse effect on eligibility for benefits.

Wider coverage, extended benefit periods, and increased benefit amounts will help society discharge its obligation to individual unemployed workers. And by maintaining more adequately their incomes and purchasing power, these measures will also buttress the economy's built-in defenses against recession. Temporary extensions of unemployment compensation benefits have been voted by the Congress during the last two recessions. It is time now for permanent legislation to bring this well-tested stabilizer more smoothly into operation when economic activity declines.

In combination, these three measures will enable Federal fiscal policy to respond, firmly, flexibly, and swiftly to oncoming recessions. Working together on this bold program, the Congress and the Executive can make an unprecedented contribution to economic stability, one that will richly reward us in fuller employment and more sustained growth, and thus, in greater human well-being and greater national strength. . . .

The momentum of our economy has been restored. This momentum must be maintained, if the full potential of our free economy is to be released in the service of the Nation and the world. In this Report I have proposed a program to sustain our prosperity and accelerate our growth—in short, to realize our economic potential. In this undertaking, I ask the support of the Congress and the American people.

The Rule of Law

F. A. HAYEK

F. A. Hayek, professor of economics at the University of Freiburg, formerly of the University of Chicago, provided some second thoughts in his famous Road to Serfdom *(1944). In the chapter reproduced here his fundamental concern is: How can democratic government hope to achieve its policy goals and still remain true to the higher requirement that just government operate according to general rules known to all well in advance of action?*

NOTHING distinguishes more clearly conditions in a free country from those in a country under arbitrary government than the observance in the former of the great principles known as the Rule of Law. Stripped of all technicalities, this means that government in all its actions is bound by rules fixed and announced beforehand—rules which make it possible to foresee with fair certainty how the authority will use its coercive powers in given circumstances and to plan one's individual affairs on the basis of this knowledge. Though this ideal can never be perfectly achieved, since legislators as well as those to whom the administration of the law is intrusted are fallible men, the essential point, that the discretion left to the executive organs wielding coercive power should be reduced as much as possible, is clear enough. While every law restricts individual freedom to some extent by altering the means which people may use in the pursuit of their aims, under the Rule of Law the government is prevented from stultifying individual efforts by *ad hoc* action. Within the known rules of the game the individual is free to pursue his personal ends and desires, certain that the powers of government will not be used deliberately to frustrate his efforts.

The distinction between the creation of a permanent framework of laws within which the productive activity is guided by individual decisions and the direction of economic activity by a central authority is thus really a particular case of the more general distinction between the Rule of Law and arbitrary government. Under the first the government confines itself to fixing rules determining the conditions under which the available resources may be used, leaving to the individuals the decision for what ends they are to be used. Under the second the government directs the use of the means of production to particular ends. The first type of rules can be made in advance, in the shape of *formal rules* which do not aim at the wants and needs of particular people. They are intended to be merely instrumental in the pursuit of people's various individual ends. And they are, or ought to be, intended for such long periods that it is impossible to know whether they will assist particular people more than others. They could almost be described as a kind of instrument of production, helping people to predict the behavior of those with whom they must collaborate, rather than as efforts toward the satisfaction of particular needs.

Economic planning of the collectivist kind necessarily involves the very opposite of this. The planning authority cannot confine itself to providing opportunities for unknown people to make whatever use of them they like. It cannot tie itself down in advance to general and formal rules which prevent arbitrariness. It must provide for the actual needs of people as they arise and then choose deliberately between them. It must constantly decide questions which cannot be answered by formal principles only, and, in making these decisions, it must set up distinctions of merit between the needs of different people. When the government has to decide how many pigs are to be raised or how many busses are to be run, which coal mines are to operate, or at what prices shoes are to be sold, these decisions cannot be deduced from formal principles or settled for long periods in advance. They depend inevitably on the circumstances of the moment, and, in making such decisions, it will always be necessary to balance one against the other the interests of various persons and groups. In the end somebody's views will have to decide whose interests are more important; and these views must become part of the law of the land, a new distinction of rank which the coercive apparatus of government imposes upon the people.

The distinction we have just used between formal law or justice and substantive rules is very important and at the same time most difficult to draw precisely in practice. Yet the general principle involved is simple enough. The difference between the two kinds of rules is the same as that between laying down a rule of the road, as in the Highway Code, and ordering people where to go; or, better still, between providing signposts and commanding people which road to take. The formal rules tell people in advance what action the state will take in certain types of situation, defined in general terms, without reference to time and place or particular people. They refer to typical situations into which anyone may get and in which the existence of such rules will be useful for a great variety of individual purposes. The knowledge that in such situations the state will act in a definite way, or require people to behave in a certain manner, is provided as a means for people to use in making their own plans. Formal rules are thus merely instrumental in the sense that they are expected to be useful to yet unknown people, for purposes for which these people will decide to use them, and in circumstances which cannot be foreseen in detail. In fact, that we do *not* know their concrete effect, that we do *not* know what particular ends these rules will further, or which particular people they will assist, that they are merely given the form most likely on the whole to benefit all the people affected by them, is the most important criterion of formal rules in the sense in which we here use this term. They do not involve a choice between particular ends or particular people, because we just cannot know beforehand by whom and in what they will be used.

In our age, with its passion for conscious control of everything, it may appear paradoxical to claim as a virtue that under one system we shall know less about the particular effect of the measures the state takes than would be true under most other systems and that a method of social control should be deemed superior because of our ignorance of its precise results. Yet this consideration is in fact the rationale of the great liberal principle of the Rule of Law. And the apparent paradox dissolves rapidly when we follow the argument a little further.

This argument is twofold; the first is economic and can here only briefly be stated. The state should confine itself to establishing rules applying to general types of situations and should allow the individuals freedom in everything which depends on the circumstances of time and place, because only the individuals concerned in each instance can fully know these circumstances and adapt their actions to them. If the individuals are to be able to use their knowledge effectively in making plans, they must be able to predict actions of the state which may affect these plans. But if the actions of the state are to be predictable, they must be determined by rules fixed independently of the concrete circumstances which can be neither foreseen nor taken into account beforehand; and the particular effects of such actions will be unpredictable. If, on the other hand, the state were to direct the individual's actions so as to achieve particular ends, its action would have to be decided on the basis of the full circumstances of the moment and would therefore be unpredictable. Hence the familiar fact that the more the state "plans," the more difficult planning becomes for the individual.

The second, moral or political, argument is even more directly relevant to the point under discussion. If the state is precisely to foresee the incidence of its actions, it means that it can leave those affected no choice. Wherever the state can exactly foresee the effects on particular people of alternative courses of action, it is also the state which chooses between the different ends. If we want to create new opportunities open to all, to offer chances of which people can make what use they like, the precise results cannot be foreseen. General rules, genuine laws as distinguished from specific orders, must therefore be intended to operate in circumstances which cannot be foreseen in detail and, therefore, their effect on particular ends or particular people cannot be known beforehand. It is in this sense alone that it is at all possible for the legislator to be impartial. To be impartial means to have no answer to certain questions—to the kind of questions which, if we have to decide them, we decide by tossing a coin. In a world where everything was precisely foreseen, the state could hardly do anything and remain impartial.

Where the precise effects of government policy on particular people are known, where the government aims directly at such particular effects, it cannot help knowing these effects, and therefore it cannot be impartial. It must, of necessity, take sides, impose its valuations upon people and, instead of assisting them in the advancement of their own ends, choose the ends for them. As soon as the particular effects are foreseen at the time a law is made, it ceases to be a mere instrument to be used by the people and becomes instead an instrument used by the lawgiver upon the people and for his ends. The state ceases to be a piece of utilitarian machinery intended to help individuals in the fullest development of their individual personality and becomes a "moral" institution—where "moral" is not used in contrast to immoral but describes an institution which imposes on its members its views on all moral questions, whether these views be moral or highly immoral. In this sense the Nazi or any other collectivist state is "moral," while the liberal state is not.

Perhaps it will be said that all this raises no serious problem because in the kind of questions which the economic planner would have to decide he need not and should not be guided by his individual prejudices but could rely on the general conviction of what is fair and reasonable. This contention usually receives support from those who have experience of planning in a particular industry and who find that there is no insuperable difficulty about arriving at a decision which all those immediately interested will accept as fair. The reason why this experience proves nothing is, of course, the selection of the "interests" concerned when planning is confined to a particular industry. Those most immediately interested in a particular issue are not necessarily the best judges of the interests of society as a whole. To take only the most characteristic case: when capital and labor in an industry agree on some policy of restriction and thus exploit the consumers, there is usually no difficulty about the division of the spoils in proportion to former earnings or on some similar principle. The loss which is divided between thousands or millions is usually either simply disregarded or quite inadequately considered. If we want to test the usefulness of the principle of "fairness" in deciding the kind of issues which arise in economic planning, we must apply it to some question where the gains and the losses are seen equally clearly. In such instances it is readily recognized that no general principle such as fairness can provide an answer. When we have to choose between higher wages for nurses or doctors and more extensive services for the sick, more milk for children and better wages for agricultural workers, or between employment for the unemployed or better wages for those already employed, nothing short of a complete system of values in which every want of every person or group has a definite place is necessary to provide an answer.

In fact, as planning becomes more and more extensive, it becomes regularly necessary to qualify legal provisions increasingly by reference to what is "fair" or "reasonable"; this means that it becomes necessary to leave the decision of the concrete case more and more to the discretion of the judge or authority in question. One could write a history of the decline of the Rule of Law, the disappearance of the *Rechtsstaat* [a state in which law prevails], in terms of the progressive introduction of these vague formulas into legislation and jurisdiction, and of the increasing arbitrariness and uncertainty of, and the consequent disrespect for, the law and the judicature, which in these circumstances could not but become an instrument of policy. It is important to point out once more in this connection that this process of the decline of the Rule of Law had been going on steadily in Germany for some time before Hitler came into power and that a policy well advanced toward totalitarian planning had already done a great deal of the work which Hitler completed.

There can be no doubt that planning necessarily involves deliberate discrimination between particular needs of different people, and allowing one man to do what another must be prevented from doing. It must lay down by a legal rule how well off particular people shall be and what different people are to be allowed to have and do. It means in effect a return to the rule of status, a reversal of the "movement of progressive societies" which, in the famous phrase of Sir Henry Maine, "has hitherto been a movement from status to contract." Indeed, the Rule of Law, more than the rule of contract, should probably be regarded as the true opposite of the rule of status. It is the Rule of

Law, in the sense of the rule of formal law, the absence of legal privileges of particular people designated by authority, which safeguards that equality before the law which is the opposite of arbitrary government.

A necessary, and only apparently paradoxical, result of this is that formal equality before the law is in conflict, and in fact incompatible, with any activity of the government deliberately aiming at material or substantive equality of different people, and that any policy aiming directly at a substantive ideal of distributive justice must lead to the destruction of the Rule of Law. To produce the same result for different people, it is necessary to treat them differently. To give different people the same objective opportunities is not to give them the same subjective chance. It cannot be denied that the Rule of Law produces economic inequality—all that can be claimed for it is that this inequality is not designed to affect particular people in a particular way. It is very significant and characteristic that socialists (and Nazis) have always protested against "merely" formal justice, that they have always objected to a law which had no views on how well off particular people ought to be, and that they have always demanded a "socialization of the law," attacked the independence of judges, and at the same time given their support to all such movements as the *Freirechtsschule* which undermined the Rule of Law.

It may even be said that for the Rule of Law to be effective it is more important that there should be a rule applied always without exceptions than what this rule is. Often the content of the rule is indeed of minor importance, provided the same rule is universally enforced. To revert to a former example: it does not matter whether we all drive on the left- or on the right-hand side of the road so long as we all do the same. The important thing is that the rule enables us to predict other people's behavior correctly, and this requires that it should apply to all cases— even if in a particular instance we feel it to be unjust.

The conflict between formal justice and formal equality before the law, on the one hand, and the attempts to realize various ideals of substantive justice and equality, on the other, also accounts for the widespread confusion about the concept of "privilege" and its consequent abuse. To mention only the most important instance of this abuse—the application of the term "privilege" to property as such. It would indeed be privilege if, for example, as has sometimes been the case in the past, landed property were reserved to members of the nobility. And it is privilege if, as is true in our time, the right to produce or sell particular things is reserved to particular people designated by authority. But to call private property as such, which all can acquire under the same rules, a privilege, because only some succeed in acquiring it, is depriving the word "privilege" of its meaning.

The unpredictability of the particular effects, which is the distinguishing characteristic of the formal laws of a liberal system, is also important because it helps us to clear up another confusion about the nature of this system: the belief that its characteristic attitude is inaction of the state. The question whether the state should or should not "act" or "interfere" poses an altogether false alternative, and the term *"laissez faire"* is a highly ambiguous and misleading description of the principles on which a liberal policy is based. Of course, every state must act and every action of the state interferes with something or other. But that is not the point. The important question is whether the individual can foresee the action of the state and make use of this knowledge as a datum in forming his own plans, with the result that the state cannot control the use made of its machinery and that the individual knows precisely how far he will be protected against interference from others, or whether the state is in a position to frustrate individual efforts. The state controlling weights and measures (or preventing fraud and deception in any other way) is certainly acting, while the state permitting the use of violence, for example, by strike pickets, is inactive. Yet it is in the first case that the state observes liberal principles and in the second that it does not. Similarly with respect to most of the general and permanent rules which the state may establish with regard to production, such as building regulations or factory laws: these may be wise or unwise in the particular instance, but they do not conflict with liberal principles so long as they are intended to be permanent and are not used to favor or harm particular people. It is true that in these instances there will, apart from the long-run effects which cannot be predicted, also be short-run effects on particular people which may be clearly known. But with this kind of laws the short-run effects are in general not (or at least ought not to be) the guiding consideration. As these immediate and predictable effects become more important compared with the long-run effects, we approach the border line where the distinction, however clear in principle, becomes blurred in practice.

The Rule of Law was consciously evolved only during the liberal age and is one of its greatest achievements, not only as a safeguard but as the legal embodiment of freedom. As Immanuel Kant put it (and Voltaire expressed it before him in very much the same terms), "Man is free if he needs to obey no person but solely the laws." As a vague ideal it has, however, existed at least since Roman times, and during the last few centuries it has never been so seriously threatened as it is today. The idea that there is no limit to the powers of the legislator is in part a result of popular sovereignty and democratic government. It has been strengthened by the belief that, so long as all actions of the state are duly authorized by legislation, the Rule of Law will be preserved. But this is completely to misconceive the meaning of the Rule of Law. This rule has little to do with the question whether all actions of government are legal in the juridical sense. They may well be and yet not conform to the Rule of Law. The fact that someone has full legal authority to act in the way he does gives no answer to the question whether the law gives him power to act arbitrarily or whether the law prescribes unequivocally how he has to act. It may well be that Hitler has obtained his unlimited powers in a strictly constitutional manner and that whatever he does is therefore legal in the juridical sense. But who would suggest for that reason that the Rule of Law still prevails in Germany?

To say that in a planned society the Rule of Law cannot hold is, therefore, not to say that the actions of the government will not be legal or that such a society will necessarily be lawless. It means only that the use of the government's coercive powers will no longer be limited and determined by preestablished rules. The law can, and to make a central direction of economic activity possible must, legalize what to all intents and purposes remains arbitrary action. If the law says that such a board or authority may do what it pleases, anything that board or authority does is legal—but its actions are certainly not subject to the Rule of Law. By giving the government unlimited powers, the most arbitrary rule can be made legal; and in this way a democracy may set up the most complete despotism imaginable.[1]

If, however, the law is to enable authorities to direct economic life, it must give them powers to make and enforce decisions in circumstances which cannot be foreseen and on principles which cannot be stated in generic form. The consequence is that, as planning extends, the delegation of legislative powers to divers boards and authorities becomes increasingly common. When before the last war, in a case to which the late Lord Hewart has recently drawn attention, Mr. Justice Darling said that "Parliament had enacted only last year that the Board of Agriculture in acting as they did should be no more impeachable than Parliament itself," this was still a rare thing. It has since become an almost daily occurrence. Constantly the broadest powers are conferred on new authorities which, without being bound by fixed rules, have almost unlimited discretion in regulating this or that activity of the people.

The Rule of Law thus implies limits to the scope of legislation: it restricts it to the kind of general rules known as formal law and excludes legislation either directly aimed at particular people or at enabling anybody to use the coercive power of the state

1. The conflict is thus *not*, as it has often been misconceived in nineteenth-century discussions, one between liberty and law. As John Locke had already made clear, there can be no liberty without law. The conflict is between different kinds of law—law so different that it should hardly be called by the same name: one is the law of the Rule of Law, general principles laid down beforehand, the "rules of the game" which enable individuals to foresee how the coercive apparatus of the state will be used, or what he and his fellow-citizens will be allowed to do, or made to do, in stated circumstances. The other kind of law gives in effect the authority power to do what it thinks fit to do. Thus the Rule of Law could clearly not be preserved in a democracy that undertook to decide every conflict of interests not according to rules previously laid down but "on its merits."

for the purpose of such discrimination. It means, not that everything is regulated by law, but, on the contrary, that the coercive power of the state can be used only in cases defined in advance by the law and in such a way that it can be foreseen how it will be used. A particular enactment can thus infringe the Rule of Law. Anyone ready to deny this would have to contend that whether the Rule of Law prevails today in Germany, Italy, or Russia depends on whether the dictators have obtained their absolute power by constitutional means.[2]

Whether, as in some countries, the main applications of the Rule of Law are laid down in a bill of rights or in a constitutional code, or whether the principle is merely a firmly established tradition, matters comparatively little. But it will readily be seen that, whatever form it takes, any such recognized limitations of the powers of legislation imply the recognition of the inalienable right of the individual, inviolable rights of man.

It is pathetic but characteristic of the muddle into which many of our intellectuals have been led by the conflicting ideals in which they believe that a leading advocate of the most comprehensive central planning like H. G. Wells should at the same time write an ardent defense of the rights of man. The individual

2. Another illustration of an infringement of the Rule of Law by legislation is the case of the bill of attainder, familiar in the history of England. The form which the Rule of Law takes in criminal law is usually expressed by the Latin tag *nulla poena sine lege*—no punishment without a law expressly prescribing it. The essence of this rule is that the law must have existed as a general rule before the individual case arose to which it is to be applied. Nobody would argue that, when in a famous case in Henry VIII's reign Parliament resolved with respect to the Bishop of Rochester's cook that "the said Richard Rose shall be boiled to death without having the advantage of his clergy," this act was performed under the Rule of Law. But while the Rule of Law had become an essential part of criminal procedure in all liberal countries, it cannot be preserved in totalitarian regimes. There, as E. B. Ashton has well expressed it, the liberal maxim is replaced by the principle *nullun crimen sine poena*—no "crime" must remain without punishment, whether the law explicitly provides for it or not. "The rights of the state do not end with punishing law breakers. The community is entitled to whatever may seem necessary to the protection of its interests—of which observance of the law, as it stands, is only one of the more elementary requirements" (E. B. Ashton, *The Fascist, His State and Mind* [1937], p. 119). What is an infringement of "the interests of the community" is, of course, decided by the authorities.

rights which Mr. Wells hopes to preserve would inevitably obstruct the planning which he desires. To some extent he seems to realize the dilemma, and we find therefore the provisions of his proposed "Declaration of the Rights of Man" so hedged about with qualifications that they lose all significance. While, for instance, his declaration proclaims that every man "shall have the right to buy and sell without any discriminatory restrictions anything which may be lawfully bought and sold," which is admirable, he immediately proceeds to make the whole provision nugatory by adding that it applies only to buying and selling "in such quantities and with such reservations as are compatible with the common welfare." But since, of course, all restrictions ever imposed upon buying or selling anything are supposed to be necessary in the interest of the "common welfare," there is really no restriction which this clause effectively prevents and no right of the individual that is safeguarded by it.

Or, to take another basic clause, the declaration states that every man "may engage in any lawful occupation" and that "he is entitled to paid employment and to a free choice whenever there is any variety of employment open to him." It is not stated, however, who is to decide whether a particular employment is "open" to a particular person, and the added provision that "he may suggest employment for himself and have his claim publicly considered, accepted or dismissed," shows that Mr. Wells is thinking in terms of an authority which decides whether a man is "entitled" to a particular position—which certainly means the opposite of free choice of occupation. And how in a planned world "freedom of travel and migration" is to be secured when not only the means of communication and currencies are controlled but also the location of industries planned, or how the freedom of the press is to be safeguarded when the supply of paper and all the channels of distribution are controlled by the planning authority, are questions to which Mr. Wells provides as little answer as any other planner.

In this respect much more consistency is shown by the more numerous reformers who, ever since the beginning of the socialist movement, have attacked the "metaphysical" idea of individual rights and insisted that in a rationally ordered world there will be no individual rights but only individual duties. This, indeed, has become the much more common attitude of our so-called "progressives," and few things are more certain to expose one to the reproach of being a reactionary than if one protects against a measure on the grounds that it is a violation of the rights of the individual. Even a liberal paper like the *Economist* was a few years ago holding up to us the example of the French, of all people, who had learned the lesson that "democratic government no less than dictatorship must always [*sic*] have plenary powers *in posse,* without sacrificing their democratic and representative character. There is no restrictive penumbra of individual rights that can never be touched by government in administrative matters whatever the circumstances. There is no limit to the power of ruling which can and should be taken by a government freely chosen by the people and can be fully and openly criticised by an opposition."

This may be inevitable in wartime, when, of course, even free and open criticism is necessarily restricted. But the "always" in the statement quoted does not suggest that the *Economist* regards it as a regrettable wartime necessity. Yet as a permanent institution this view is certainly incompatible with the preservation of the Rule of Law, and it leads straight to the totalitarian state. It is, however, the view which all those who want the government to direct economic life must hold.

How even a formal recognition of individual rights, or of the equal rights of minorities, loses all significance in a state which embarks on a complete control of economic life, has been amply demonstrated by the experience of the various Central European countries. It has been shown there that it is possible to pursue a policy of ruthless discrimination against national minorities by the use of recognized instruments of economic policy without ever infringing the letter of the statutory protection of minority rights. This oppression by means of economic policy was greatly facilitated by the fact that particular industries or activities were largely in the hands of a national minority, so that many a measure aimed ostensibly against an industry or class was in fact aimed at a national minority. But the almost boundless possibilities for a policy of discrimination and oppres-

The Roosevelt Revolution

MARIO EINAUDI

*Professor Einaudi of Cornell University provided probably the
best insights on the political economy of the New Deal in* The
Roosevelt Revolution *(1959), of which the following essay is a
concluding part. Did the New Deal prove Tocqueville's forecast
wrong? Does the New Deal prove that democratic government can
be pro-equality, maintain freedom, be dynamic, and yet be pro-
capitalist too?*

IN TOCQUEVILLE's *Democracy in America,* the issues of presidential power, federal government, and continuity pale by comparison
with the question: How can freedom survive in a democracy?
And to this question we now turn. . . .

Tocqueville had no illusions about the advance of the equali-
tarian movement, to him the essence of democracy. Equality of
status was the basic fact of modern times everywhere in the
Western world. Democracy, conceived as equality, was both inevitable and desirable, in spite of the longings of Tocqueville for
the aristocratic societies of the past. But there was no surrender
in his mind of the power of man to determine the course of
history: "It is true," he says, "that around every man a fatal
circle is traced beyond which he cannot pass; but within the wide
verge of that circle he is powerful and free; as it is with man, so
it is with communities. The nations of our time cannot prevent the
conditions of men from becoming equal, but it depends upon
themselves whether the principle of equality is to lead them
to servitude or freedom, to knowledge or barbarism, to prosperity or wretchedness."

This, then, was the problem to which Tocqueville addressed
himself: the problem of the survival of the individual, with his
rights, in a democratic society where the essential doctrine was

that of the rule of the majority, of a majority which, no matter how formed and by what issues, viewing itself as the *major pars* in numbers and wisdom, would strive to assert itself and to stamp out the minority.

With Europe seething with unrest, with France starting on its journey of moral corruption under the July monarchy and unable to find the pivot around which to hinge her political system, Tocqueville saw the need of starting an inquiry into the sources of strength and weakness of the greatest of the democracies operating under ideal conditions, American democracy. For here he might find the answer to the question uppermost in his thoughts.

Once possessed of the answer, Tocqueville imagined himself ready to advise his countrymen and to help a democratic France and Europe to follow the path of freedom rather than that of despotism. This, then, was his objective.

With this in mind, how did American democracy appear to Tocqueville?

In America, as in Europe, the pressure of the majority was becoming stronger. Most of the state constitutions were fostering the absolute sovereignty of the majority with artificial means. Elected for brief terms, legislators were laboring under the weight of direct mandates from the electors. Laws were uncertain and short-lived, and so were the constitutions, subject to continuous change. "This omnipotence of the majority," continues Tocqueville, "and the rapid as well as absolute manner in which its decisions are executed in the United States, not only render the law unstable, but exercise the same influence upon the execution of the law and the conduct of the administration. As the majority is the only power that it is important to court, all its projects are taken up with the greatest ardor; but no sooner is its attention distracted, than all this ardor ceases."

Tocqueville thought that, as a result, the individual would suffer and often be left without any redress for wrongs suffered. He foresaw the danger of tyranny because public opinion, legislative powers, and executive powers were each only different manifestations of the same majority which had inflicted the wrong. But he was underestimating the ultimate power of the federal judiciary in taking over the protection of the rights of freedom, and one can lament his readiness to envisage the coming about of a multitude of petty tyrannies before which the federal Constitution and government would be helpless, in spite of his noble vision of the federal Union.

Developing rapidly in a country in which democracy was flourishing was a new and harsh aristocracy, identified by Tocqueville as the aristocracy of industry. The danger was that this business class would first impoverish and debase the men working under it and then abandon them to the charity of the public. Tocqueville had no doubt concerning the vigor with which the industrial classes would pursue their goals of innovation and expansion. Nor did he have any doubts of the means they would use in order to gain their objectives, nor, finally, of the way with which they would meet the difficulties they were creating. He thought that the American experience would differ little from the European one in its human consequences, and that the trail of the industrial revolution would often be one of despair, even though he saw in the United States a greater participation of the people in industry and a greater cooperation between the poorest and the most opulent members of the commonwealth. The spirit of adventure and of risk-taking is exposing Americans to "unexpected and formidable embarrassments. . . . As they are all more or less engaged in productive industry, at the least shock given to business all private fortunes are put into jeopardy at the same time, and the state is shaken."

Tocqueville remains one of the earliest critical commentators of our industrial age to have seen the problems of business controls over the community, and the dangers of the probable failure of the industrial classes to accept the responsibilities that went with power and to which earlier aristocracies had submitted. To have also suggested that America would face greater hardships than other countries because of the urgency that manufacturing and industrial activities had assumed in the country represents a remarkable feat of prophecy.

Most of the trends forecast by Tocqueville came true in the next century. The rise of America's industrial power was indeed phenomenal, and the state was "shaken" in 1929. The vitality of

American democracy which Tocqueville had felt joined hands with constitutionalism to subdue the industrial monster to the medium of constitutional principle, to use Harold Laski's words. And this may well be listed as one of the permanent accomplishments of the Roosevelt Revolution.

For our time, there is added significance in the broad outlines of American economic policy since 1932. It is the demonstration of the irrelevance of the theories and practices of the Soviet revolution in the affairs of an industrialized society. The demonstration was not an easy one nor was its success expected with confidence by everybody. There have been many and persistent voices in the West bent upon proving our indebtedness to Russia in so far as planning and state intervention were concerned. The belief that the Soviet pattern of action had to be applied in times of trouble was an ingrained one. It took John Maynard Keynes's eloquence and theoretical constructions and Franklin Delano Roosevelt's practical political manipulations to provide proof of the inapplicability of the Soviet experience to the West and to give evidence of the bottomless gap between the enforced-slave drive to industrialize a peasant society at full speed and regardless of cost, and the delicate task of assuring the continued free growth of a highly industrialized nation, some of whose means of production were idle.

What stood out at the end of the 1932–1952 period was that the United States could face its day of reckoning, not with verbally simple and fetching formulas such as expropriation or nationalization, or forced savings, or directed labor, or central and total government planning and investment, but with other policies, less easily reducible to ideological generalizations, but which succeeded in effect in reconciling tradition and contemporary realities, the ideals of individual and of community action, those of free and public enterprise.

Government intervention was limited and selective. It aimed at freeing, not freezing, economic life. It fought private monopolistic rule over the welfare of man (what Roosevelt called "private socialism") and replaced it, to some extent at least, with the more distant benevolence of public oversight. It showed by example what private activity should be, and faded away when private business was ready to do the job. It moved into the higher financial reaches to restore to capitalism the freedom and responsibility it had lost. It demonstrated that a strong public hand did not mean exclusion of private efforts. It viewed under a fresh light the old disputes about property rights and, against the Marxist doctrine, it made clear the possibility of bringing to private property a sense of its duty to the community at large, without interfering at all with its formal structure. Property could be chastised and yet kept alive.

In the contest of Keynes versus Marx, the New Deal sided with Keynes (perhaps without realizing it) and sent Marx tumbling down. It has been difficult ever since to put Marxism together again as a revolutionary doctrine within a mature industrial society. The fact that in the United States some large private economic enterprises do exist and that they certainly do move toward forms of "social" exercise of their functions does not vindicate Marxism at all. For too many other conditions of freedom and types of individual and group activities are in being as countervailing factors. American economic life has not become a narrow, one-way street. Communist theoreticians know this to be true and are giving increasing signs of restlessness when looking at the "unexplainable" developments of the American economy. Instead of the unbearable tensions that ought to be present at this moment of history, preceding as it does in the Marxist mythology the final catastrophe of the capitalistic system—instead of the one supreme, commanding will that Marx envisaged as a necessity in a system of such complexity—America shows narrowing social cleavages and all the characteristics of a pluralistic society.

But even in 1835, in spite of the difficulties to which he was pointing, Tocqueville was confident that in America democracy would not suffocate freedom. Democracy had indeed been successful, while at the same time freedom had been able to maintain itself. Customs, legal habits, decentralization, and physical conditions account, in Tocqueville's judgment, for this happy combination. . . .

AMERICA AND UTOPIA

Democracy, then, was good, and it was here to stay. And as a result of the historical process he had unraveled with such perspicacity, Tocqueville knew that it would have been idle to imagine a return to traditional absolutism were free democracy to fail. Princes were called tyrants, but religion, local autonomies, and traditions limited their powers. "Princes had the right, but they had neither the means nor the desire of doing whatever they pleased." With the flattening of the intermediate structures of the old regimes, under the urge toward equality and uniformity, a new oppression, which the traditional concepts of despotism and tyranny would be inadequate to define, would arise, were the balance lost between freedom and democracy.

Tocqueville offers a memorable description of democratic despotism. . . . The question was how to avoid this destructive and all-pervasive tyranny over men, for which we have today found a name.

Contemporary American democracy is not Utopian and is not totalitarian. It is planted in common sense, in the realm of the possible, in freedom.

America is not Utopia. The confidence in the political process often shown by these pages has not been meant to convey the belief that all is well with America and that somehow the American people, presumably endowed with higher rational faculties, have been able to do what other peoples have failed to do—that Americans have at long last embarked upon the journey to which everybody aspires, to that never-never land of milk and honey and diamonds described by eighteenth-century travelers.

Utopia could not be born in the middle of the twentieth century, amid the ugliness of our industrial civilizations, the terrors of the atomic age, and the desperate confrontation of the old Western way of life with the new ways of life of the East. It can hardly even be conceived as a distant image, in times filled with dismay and waiting. The present itself in the United States is complicated and critical enough to make one feel that the country is still a long way this side of Utopia.

There is the sadness of the cities, showing so clearly the failure of man to relate growth to beauty. There is the bitterness of race relations as the two camps see sweeping change approaching, but are not yet prepared to accept its consequences. There is the impersonality of large areas of human activities with its dampening effect on man's freedom; the cumulative accretion of power to the bureaucracies, both public and private, managing them; the weight of the use of public funds for nonproductive purposes.

There is still poverty, more shocking because we do not seem to know what to do about it. The poor are no longer the submerged one-third of the 1930's, but their far smaller clusters appear irreducible and pose a challenge which is still beyond the comprehension of the country. There is the problem of what to do with what we produce. And there is the appalling gap between aesthetic values and material gadgets, essential social needs and the way in which the economic effort of the country is spent.

There is the all too visible leveling of habits, the conformity and the aiming at the average. Even though the rich are not very noticeable in the sea of prosperity, they still have great privileges and power as well as the ability to control their own affairs regardless of the interests of others.

It is conceivable, as Robert Hutchins has suggested, that large numbers of Americans, spoiled by industrialism and success, no longer want to be, or can be, free. It is true, as Arthur Schlesinger has said, that there is a surfeit of official piety.

But America is not today, nor is it likely to become tomorrow, a totalitarian democracy, nor a garrison state, nor a police state. America is a democratic and individualistic society which, showing the ugly scars of modern mass-production civilization, has retained faith in the human beings that make it up. As constitutionalism, defined as the regulated application of humane and rational faculties to the task of guiding the political community toward common goals in an atmosphere that will recognize the supreme moral values inherent in the individual, declines elsewhere, it still retains the upper hand in the United States.

What we have witnessed since 1933—a time of despair and gloom, a time when by all contemporary evidence the political processes the West had applied during its period of growth and expansion in the preceding centuries appeared doomed—has been the recovery and the use of power by democratic leaders who, without rigid ideology and tyranny, yet with a broad conception of the needs of the times, have succeeded in renovating the historical heritage of the United States while maintaining freedom.

What we have seen in the United States has been the systematic and inventive search for solutions to the difficulties of industrial mass democracy, a search intended to realize the ideals of community without collectivism, the ideal of freedom without anarchy, the advantages of technology without the loss of humanism. The managers have had their day in the United States. But they have been kept in check and have not taken over the country.

What the Roosevelt Revolution has done has been to keep the door open so as to permit to our generation a chance to decide in liberty what we must do. The United States can today do so, on a higher platform of welfare and happiness and real freedom than ever before. When we look around us, we see throughout the world peoples whose doors toward the future are controlled by irresponsible elites now making all the decisions. America is still free, I believe, to choose among alternatives and to make up its mind to a large extent as to what it wants. In 1932, there was a strong chance that this would not be possible for long. The Roosevelt Revolution, having brought together common action and individual liberty, has preserved that freedom. This is bound to be the verdict of history.

The Making of the Issues—1964

THEODORE H. WHITE

In The Making of the President 1964, *Theodore H. White sees the Johnson-Goldwater campaign as a watershed in American politics. Among other things, it seems to have brought back the "great issues" after a pragmatic interlude of over a generation. This he discusses in Chapter 10, reproduced here.*

THE CAMPAIGN of 1964 was that rare thing in American political history, a campaign based on issues.

War and peace; the nature and role of government; the morality and mercy of society; the quality of life—all were discussed in a campaign that will leave its mark behind in American life for a generation. A myriad cross-currents of conscience, judgment and tradition were engaged in the voter choice of 1964—but they were cross-currents resolved in individual decisions in solitary voting booths, and the massive totals of the late fall tally gave little indication of how much and how deeply Americans had been stirred to think. . . .

Up and down the nation, at prop stop and whistle stop, by dawn and dusk and at high noon, Barry Goldwater first challenged and then, as November approached, grieved: "What kind of country do we want to have?"—and to this challenge Lyndon Johnson replied in as masterful a campaign as the Democrats have ever conducted. A hundred million Americans were asked to hear the two leaders give their vision of America, as if they were citizens of a Greek *polis* two thousand years before; and rarely, when questions were asked about the nature of fate and country, have citizens heard their leaders give answers so violently and unequivocally opposed. . . .

For thirty years Republicans and Democrats had fought each other in the arena of the center, where their differences, though

185

real, were small, narrow or administrative—differences of pace, posture and management in a direction that both parties alike pursued. Goldwater, however, proposed to give the nation a choice, not an echo—and not just one choice but a whole series of choices, a whole system of ideas which clashed with the governing ideas that had ruled America for a generation: a choice on nuclear weapons, a choice on defense posture, a choice on the treatment of Negroes, a choice on dealing with Communism, a choice on the nature of central government. There were many choices, but the rub was that no voter could pick at will among those choices. A voter must buy the entire Goldwater package of ideas—or reject them entirely. He could choose America as it was moving, in the direction it was moving, in full tide of power and prosperity—or he must choose to reverse the direction entirely. In Goldwater, one had to take all or nothing. . . .

What exactly were the issues? What precisely were the choices offered in 1964? How valid were they? How did the craftsmen of politics convert these ideas technically and politically into the emotions which move American voters to vote? How ephemeral or how permanent will they prove in the future to be?

There is no doubt in the mind of any candidate, any political observer or any man who trooped the long marches from coast to coast with both candidates that one primordial issue overshadowed all others: the problem of War and Peace, pegged on America's use of its arsenal of nuclear weapons.

How, when, by whose authority, where should such weapons be used? . . .

What exactly had Goldwater said? And what exactly did Goldwater mean? . . .

Did Goldwater mean that any tactical unit commander could use the weapons of holocaust? Under what circumstances? To destroy a bridge? Or an enemy concentration? Or a city? And if so—who then held the trigger on the implacable escalation of destruction? . . .

The issue, in short, was not at what technical level nuclear weapons would be unleashed or which general might make command decisions.

The issue, as it rose steaming into politics and as deftly molded by the Democrats, was quite valid: Just what attitude *should* Americans take toward the use of nuclear power? How ready should government, as a whole, be to use nuclear weapons and risk the escalation to destruction?

The issue was never, as Democrats tried to define it to their advantage, a choice between war and peace. But it *was* a choice, nonetheless—between peace and risk of war . . . none of the stabbing slogans that blossomed in the wake of Goldwater's journeyings ever caught the essence of this prime issue as did the one suggested to the Democratic National Committee by an anonymous North Carolinian: IN YOUR HEART, YOU KNOW HE MIGHT, read the last of the variations on the enigmatic Goldwater catch phrase. And in the end, because they had been persuaded that indeed he *might,* millions of Americans voted against the Republican.

Goldwater's second great issue was an equally complicated one, equally overlaid with subtleties that had to be violated with a crude yes or no vote: this was his crusade against the central government—against an all-dominating, all-entangling Federal bureaucracy of Washington. Whenever a political reporter journeys with a Republican candidate—right, left or center—he knows the one sure-fire catch line is the attack on the government in Washington. All Republicans praise the flag—and denounce the government.

A shrewd candidate has, indeed, a very sound and forward-ringing issue in denunciation of this centralization—if he handles it skillfully. The American government is, to a large extent, stone-hardened in fossil structures and fossil theories that descend to it from the days of the New Deal emergency thirty years ago, too many of which have outlived their usefulness and hinder, rather than help, the bursting new society Americans have made.

Yet how to remove these fossil relics from American life is today one of the most technically complicated problems both of government and of politics. . . .

All Americans, generally and as a matter of principle, will denounce distant Federal paternalism—but will scream if any tampering threatens the benefits which they personally get out of it. Thus, the roar that comes when any speaker denounces the distant Federal Government is a heartfelt response. Yet when the meeting is over and the hearers wander away to examine the general proposition, they very frequently have second thoughts; for what the other fellow calls a subsidy may seem to him a constitutional guarantee against need; what cramps one man is another's crutch; restrictions placed on one individual guarantee someone else's freedom; one man's open cook-out pit is someone else's smog; and the boss's annoyance with the paper that clutters his desk is balanced by his secretary's need for unemployment insurance.

The problems of governing a technological civilization like America are complicated enough in themselves. But they are fused by emotion into a general resentment of all forms of increasingly impersonal control over an increasingly accelerating complexity. . . . And to all of these confused emotions a final exasperation is added by the new Supreme Court—a Supreme Court which has abandoned the old concept of the judiciary as a balance wheel against excess, and replaced it by a concept of the judiciary as a propulsive wheel that speeds Washington faster and faster—from abolition of school prayers in village schoolhouses to legislative reapportionment.

For these confused emotions, no man over the years has been a more perfect voice than Barry Goldwater. Over the years he has denounced farm subsidies outright; advocated the abolition of Rural Electrification; urged the selling of TVA; indicted the National Labor Relations Board; excoriated the Supreme Court; riddled the bureaucracy with scorn and contempt. When over and over again during the campaign he would promise, "I will give you back your freedom," his sincerity would evoke the wildest response. His misfortune was that he could not make clear just how, and by what degrees, he would free the American people from paternalism and central government without exposing them at the same time to some personal loss.

It was here, in his confusion, that the Democrats lanced him. Out of the vast mass of his many statements and speeches, they chose to hook and hang him on one issue: Social Security.

Goldwater was general in his denunciation of big government; the Democrats chose a specific for response, and they could not have chosen better.

Of all the enterprises of big government, none except the income tax touches more people than Social Security. But whereas the income tax takes, Social Security gives. In 1964 the Social Security system paid out more than $19 billion to recipients of its insurance; in February of 1964 over 19 million people received its old-age or disability benefits—and another 90 million people had "insured status" with the Social Security from which they expected, in their turn, someday to draw a benefit.

To attack Social Security is thus, in the highest political sense, dangerous. Nor did Goldwater ever attack it—just as, indeed, he never demanded war. What he did instead was to ruminate aloud about what might be done with it—just as he ruminated out loud about the use of nuclear weapons. . . .

Republicans (and Democrats too) might recognize that the vast and tangled jungle growth of Federal bureaucracy is a menace to American values and American options; but if, as his opponents—Rockefeller, Scranton, Johnson and Humphrey—were quick to point out, it meant forfeiting their Social Security, what then? It was all too clear, even early in the campaign, that millions of modest Republicans in retirement—in southern California, in Florida, in New Hampshire, in Pennsylvania—were unwilling to risk those monthly checks that could run from as little as $40 to a maximum of $254 for a family.

And, again, the subtleties of the great issue of central government versus local or private initiative could not be separated out. Again, on this issue as on the bomb issue, America had to answer yes or no.

These were the issues that translated best, however coarsely, into the campaign clash. But there were other issues, equally weighty, with which neither of the candidates could grapple because these issues were even more subtle, even more complicated.

The issue of civil rights was as central to American concerns in the campaign of 1964 as the issue of war and peace.

Yet both candidates jointly decided to exclude from the campaign dialogue as far as possible any implied appeal to racism—and, accepting this exclusion with high principle and great responsibility, Goldwater took the loss.

Goldwater had, of course, begun by painting himself into a corner on this issue too. He had, out of conviction, voted against the Civil Rights Bill in June—against the warnings, it must be noted, of his political advisers. Thus he had pinpointed himself as the outright anti-Negro candidate of the campaign, clearly on record in an area where the decisive morality of America was against him. Now the exclusion agreement cramped him in exploring the subtleties and shadings of this morality.

The subtleties and shadings of white morality on the problem of Negroes are most realistically examined by the coarse measurement of politicians at the three rungs in the ladder of fundamental Negro need: jobs, housing and education.

Generally, across the country, politicians know that their white voters will accept Negroes as equals on the job—or, at least, as entitled to equal opportunity on the job. There is little danger of serious backlash at this first level of demand. No Congressman who voted *for* the Civil Rights Bill in 1964 was defeated for re-election; eleven of the twenty-two Northern Congressmen who voted *against* it did suffer defeat.

The next level of Negro demand, housing, is more dangerous; in general, if politicians can keep the issue within their city councils or at a deputized level, they will vote for open-housing ordinances; yet they know that when the issue has been brought to the people by open popular referendum, the people invariably, without exception, have voted against open-housing laws.

The final level, education, is the flash point of peril. Politicans everywhere flee involvement in the integration of schools as if it were instant contamination. . . .

What is involved in the present development of the civil-rights problem in America is the nature of all the silent, unrecognized neighborhood and ethnic communities that make up American urban life. The morality of the Civil Rights Act of 1964—and the absolute political need for it—cannot be questioned. But the next question—which the campaign of 1964 might have illuminated, but did not—is how men once freed for civil equality in the general forum of employment, opportunity and politics shall go about living together, or apart, in communities of their own choosing.

This, along with war and peace, was a central issue of the campaign of 1964. . . .

But the race issue as such, a cardinal manipulant of emotions, was left buried—left to work its own results in the states of the South that Goldwater carried. And left to work its way silently in the big cities, where the white workingman took out his fears on local candidates who threatened to open and perhaps destroy his neighborhood—but in his national choice, forced to buy either the Johnson package or the Goldwater package, chose Johnson.

There remained, finally, an area of contention and difference that is so new it still lacks an appropriate name. One can call it, perhaps, the issue of quality. Quality was what John F. Kennedy was all about, in its classic, Greek sense—how to live with grace and intelligence, with bravery and mercy. Quality was what he sought in his brief three-year administration; but it had not been an issue in his campaign of 1960, except as his personality and eloquence gave an example of it.

Yet in 1964 two men with far less of the sense of quality than John F. Kennedy succeeded, together, in making quality the fourth and last of the major issues of the campaign. Goldwater called it the "morality issue"; Johnson called it "the Great Society." During the campaign neither could define what he meant—but they were bringing into engagement what in another decade, if peace persists, may well be the central issue of American life: What is the end of man? What is his purpose on earth? How shall he conduct himself with grace and mercy and dignity? No other society in history has ever been rich enough to face such a problem or to discuss it in the political forum; quality has been something left to the church and the philosophers; all other societies have been too deeply involved with making, getting, existing, subsisting and defending themselves. Americans in the 1960s are faced for the first time with the problems of abundance—the purpose and style of life in a society whose great majority has been relieved from real want and thus freed to express itself.

There was, of course, want enough in America in 1964—and to this the Democratic candidates, Johnson and Humphrey, constantly addressed themselves in their poverty speeches and program. But this want, though real and all the more galling because of its contrast with surrounding affluence ("the prison with glass walls" is how Eric Sevareid described the condition of the poor), was less than the giant fact of prosperity. There was no doubt that John F. Kennedy and his economists had brought about the first fundamental change in American economic policy since Franklin D. Roosevelt—and the nation glowed with a boom that was one of the world's wonders. The boom terrified Europeans, angered the underdeveloped in the world, baffled the Russians. In America, in mid-campaign, the newspapers gave only scanty paragraphs to a settlement won by the automobile workers in Detroit—guaranteeing retirement to auto workers at age sixty at $100 a week; abroad, the statement could not be believed and could be taken as propaganda in a country like France, where a full colonel on active duty receives the same base pay. Luxuries undreamed of five years before were now mail-order items. A record eight million new cars were purchased; pleasure-boat sales were estimated at 400,000 a year; new dwellings were started at the rate of 1.5 million a year. The *increase* alone of America's gross national product in the four years of the Kennedy-Johnson administration was greater than the *entire* gross national product of Germany in 1964—by $122 billion to $100 billion. Wages rose, profits rose, the stock market rose, vacations lengthened. The conscientious pointed out, quite rightly, that one fifth of the nation lived in poverty. But the other four fifths *were* the majority, freed apparently from the curse of Adam and invited to contemplate their souls and identities.

This contemplation of personality had led to a strange country: it was as if a radioactive dust, called money, was in the air, invisible but everywhere, addling or mutating old habits of life. . . .

America in 1964 was a perplexing place indeed. There was no doubt that American genius was surpassing itself in all the old measures of progress. The Japanese might be abreast of America in electronics and ahead in shipbuilding; the Germans were abreast of America in steel technology, the British in motor design, the French in biologicals. But no other nation possessed such capacity over the entire range—in steel, in electronics, in instrumentation, in plastics, in automation, in computer technique, in film direction, in chemicals, in medical innovation, in any exploration of man's mastery over matter.

But did this make Americans happy? Here the evidence was varied and could be read either way. A study of suicide and mental health conducted in 1964 brought up the estimate that one in forty Americans—no less than 5 million—had attempted at one time or another to commit suicide; and the suicide rate was gently rising—from 10.1 per 100,000 (in 1954) to 11.0 (in 1963). More Americans lived longer than ever before—the number of Americans over sixty-five was estimated at over 17 million, as compared to 12.3 million in 1950. But who would care for them? Where would they live? The average sixty-five-year-old now has a life expectancy of over fourteen years. How could the agony and loneliness of old age be comforted without destroying the vitality and resources of younger families whose energies and efforts were bent on their children? Should government involve itself in the care of these aging citizens? Should a compassionate society tax itself to ease their woes, or would such a step lock citizens in another system of digits and taxes?

Goldwater's response to this unsettling experience of America was to mourn. "What's happening to us? What's happening to our America?" he would ask wherever he marched.

And here again the Democrats hanged him, not on fact but on attitude.

For what was happening was not all bad. Newspaper headlines warned of the alarming rate of dropouts from schools and colleges. But when one read the texts beneath the headlines, the statistics told another story; of 1930's fifth-graders, less than half finished high school; of 1950's, almost three fifths; of those who were in fifth grade in 1954-55, 636 per thousand had graduated from high school by 1962. Thus, the drop-out rate was falling—only the need for education was growing faster than the effort to catch up. There was, indeed, a school crisis, but whereas twenty-five years earlier only one in three high-school graduates went on to college, now more than half go to college; and their numbers had jumped from 1.5 million in 1940 to an expected 5.2 million in 1965. Americans were spending more on hard liquor—but per-capita consumption was not increasing. Americans were merely buying more expensive brands. Crime was up —yes. But not felonies. The shocking figures came in the shrinking big cities with their tensions. Overall, however, the new America was much safer than thirty years before—with murder down from 8.9 per 100,000 in 1930 to 5.1 in 1962. . . .

Johnson and Humphrey, Goldwater and Miller, all believed that the purpose of America was to enrich the individual life. Something, perhaps, was wrong with the condition of that life in 1964. But Goldwater and Miller saw what was wrong as the government; and Johnson and Humphrey saw the government as the chief means of dealing with the wrong.

Perhaps both Democrats and Republicans were wrong, as they tried to explain America to Americans; perhaps the nature of life in the abundant society requires deeper thinking than can be done in a political campaign. Yet if the approaches of both sides were unsettling to people and unsatisfying to thinkers, Goldwater managed to bring to his approach a particularly joyless quality. What the Democrats offered was offered with glee, gusto and the colors of the rosy-fingered dawn.

Goldwater could offer—and this was his greatest contribution to American politics—only a contagious concern which made people realize that indeed they must begin to think about such things. And this will be his great credit in historical terms: that finally he introduced the condition and quality of American morality and life as a subject of political debate.

Goldwater caused nerve ends to twinge with his passion and indignation. Yet he had no handle to the problems, no program, no solution—except backward to the Bible and the God of the desert. Fiercely proud of his sturdy grandfather who had struggled, fought, wandered and, by manliness, made civilization grow on the Old Frontier, he could not quite grasp the nature of the newer enemies on the new frontier of life. Proud of his handsome, clean-lined family, proud of his radiant children, proud of his family's war record and patriotism, he had in him neither the compassion nor the understanding to deal with the faceless newer enemies of the Digital Society.

These, then, were the issues—profound, moving, deeply dividing.

In 1960 either Richard M. Nixon or John F. Kennedy could well have campaigned under the other's chief slogan: Nixon could easily have bannered his campaign with "Let's Get America Moving Again," and Kennedy could easily have accepted "Keep the Peace Without Surrender." It was an inner music of the soul that separated them, an outer style of leadership which urged the Americans to the choice of 1960.

In 1964 it was otherwise.

The gap between Johnson and Goldwater was total. Though as masculine Southwest types they used the same language, the same profanities, shared the same drinking style, indulged in the same homespun metaphors, these similarities were meaningless when compared to the philosophies that separated them. . . .

Suggested Further Readings

PRIVATE LIFE: FREEDOMS, RESTRAINTS, AND CONSEQUENCES

Adams, Walter, *The Structure of American Industry* (Macmillan, 1961).
Becker, Carl, *Freedom and Responsibility in the American Way of Life* (Knopf, 1947).
Clark, J. M. *Alternative to Serfdom* (Vintage, 1960. 2nd Ed.).
Hamilton, Alexander, John Jay and James Madison, *Federalist Papers.*
Friedman, Milton, *Capitalism and Freedom* (Chicago, 1962).
Grimes, Alan P., *Equality in America* (Oxford, 1964).
Hartz, Louis, *The Liberal Tradition in America* (Harcourt, 1955).
Heilbroner, Robert, *The Worldly Philosophers* (Simon & Schuster, 1961).
Schumpeter, Joseph, *Capitalism, Socialism and Democracy* (Harper, 1942).
Vidich, Arthur, and Joseph Bensman, *Small Town in Mass Society* (Anchor, 1958).

PUBLIC ORDER: INSTITUTIONS IN CAPITALISTIC SOCIETY

Beard, Charles A., *An Economic Interpretation of the Constitution* (Macmillan, 1914).
Berle, Adolph, *The Twentieth Century Capitalist Revolution* (Harcourt, 1954).
Brady, Robert A., *Business as a System of Power* (Columbia, 1943).
Dahl, Robert A., and Charles E. Lindblom, *Politics, Economics and Welfare* (Harper, 1953).
Galbraith, J. K., *American Capitalism* (Houghton, Mifflin, 1956).
Janowitz, Morris, *The Professional Soldier* (Free Press, 1960).
Key, V. O., *Politics, Parties and Pressure Groups* (Crowell, 1964).
Mills, C. Wright, *White Collar* (Oxford, 1956).
Polanyi, Karl, *The Great Transformation* (Beacon, 1957).
Pritchett, C. Herman, *The American Constitution* (McGraw-Hill, 1959).

PUBLIC ORDER: THE ROLE OF GOVERNMENT

Adams, Walter, and Horace Gray, *Monopoly in America* (Macmillan, 1955).
Bailey, Stephen K., *Congress Makes a Law* (Columbia, 1950).
Bator, Francis, *The Question of Government Spending* (Harper, 1960).
Einaudi, Mario, *et al., Nationalization in France and Italy* (Cornell, 1955).
Fainsod, Merle, *et al., Government and the American Economy* (Norton, 1959).

Friedrich, Carl, *Constitutional Government and Democracy* (Ginn, 1950).
Lasswell, Harold D., *National Security and Individual Freedom* (McGraw-Hill, 1950).
Lippmann, Walter, *The Public Philosophy* (Mentor, 1956).
McConnell, Grant, *Private Power and American Democracy* (Knopf, 1966).
Shonfield, Andrew, *Modern Capitalism* (Oxford, 1965).

#70 #230